TAKE CHARGE

of your

TAKE CHARGE
of your
Destiny

How to Create the Life You Were Born to Live

JIM DONOVAN

For more information on foreign distribution, call
717-530-2122.
Reach us on the Internet: www.soundwisdom.com.

Sound Wisdom
P.O. Box 310
Shippensburg, PA 17257-0310

ISBN 13 TP: 978-0-7684-1046-4
ISBN 13 Ebook: 978-0-7684-1047-1

For Worldwide Distribution, Printed in the U.S.A.
2 3 4 5 6 7 8 / 19 18 17 16

FOR GOD AND THE ANGELS,

WHO HAVE WATCHED OVER

AND PROTECTED ME AND

ARE THE INSPIRATION FOR

EVERYTHING I WRITE.

Dedication

This book is dedicated to my
wife, Georgia, for her continued
encouragement and loving support.

Acknowledgments

My heartfelt thanks to my wife, Georgia, for her support of my dreams and vision and for lending her talents and editorial expertise to this book.

I want to especially thank Beth Meininger, Rob Kall, Terri Levine, Sharon Wilson, Mary Beth Spann, Sandie Pinches, Siobhan Murphy, and coaches everywhere who are making this world a better place in which to live.

Special thanks to my mastermind partner Art (Ski) Swikowski and to Jim Sutton for being in my life.

Thank you to Dave Wildasin for his friendship and his support of my writing.

Thank you to Christina Lynch, John Martin and the team at Sound Wisdom for their part in this book. Your efforts are much appreciated.

Thank you to all the people who helped make this book a fun and enjoyable experience.

Lastly, I want to thank all the readers of my books and blog who have provided me with encouragement and inspiration throughout the years. I am honored to have been a part of your lives.

Contents

Introduction

*I*f you've read any of my books, you know that I am a big proponent of designing and creating the life of your dreams.

You know I believe it is your God-given birthright to have a life of joy, happiness, health, love, fun, prosperity, excitement, abundance, and all the other wonderful things life here on this earth has to offer. To accept less is to shortchange yourself and your loved ones.

This book has been developed from the work that I have done in live seminars, workshops, and with my individual clients. I ask that you, my friend, approach reading this as if you were with me at a live event. You will be asked, from time to time, to stop reading and complete an activity or write in your journal. Please complete the simple activities, as they have been created to help you design the life that you've always wanted and have been used successfully by myself and people I've worked with.

You may want to read this book more than once and revisit the activities, especially the ones having to do with goals and visions, from time to time. As with any book, do not simply accept what is written. Test it for yourself and take from it only that which feels right for you—after all, this is your life. Remember, throughout this book that within you is the power to change your life.

Your Intention

Before we begin, I'd like you to think about your intention for reading this book. Intentions are very powerful. They send our desires out to the universe in front of us. Stop reading for a moment, and think about why you are reading this book. What do you want to take from the experience? What is your reason for taking the time to read this book in the first place? What do you want to get from it?

In my live seminars, I ask people to share why they are attending and what they intend to take from our time together. Obliviously, I cannot do that with you because you are reading this information, but I can ask you to think about what your response would be. Do you intend to simply read the book and think about what you read here or do you want more? Do you intend to take the ideas presented here, integrate them into your day-to-day life, and use them to create the life you were born to live?

Simply set your intentions for investing your time in reading this book. You may want to write something in your journal. After all, you have invested money in buying the book and will now invest a certain amount of your time, your most precious asset, in reading it. The clearer you are as to why, the more you will take from the experience.

If you have read any of my other books, you know I don't write about theory. I write from my own experiences. I know with absolute certainty that the principles, techniques, and ideas presented here work because I have used them to change my own life from one of misery and despair to living today what I can only describe as a truly magical life. I continue to apply these principles daily as my own life continues to expand, and I enjoy even more of the joy and the beauty that surrounds us.

I am truly blessed. When I pass a homeless person on the street, I always say a prayer for the unfortunate person as well as a prayer of gratitude, for I understand deeply the phrase "There, but for the grace of God, go I."

I have lived in depression, and at more than one point in my life I was without a place to call home. I have been at the bottom, gone without food for days at a time, lived in poverty, and sold most of my possessions. I once heard Anthony Robins talk about washing dishes in the bathtub because the room where he lived had no sink, and I laughed because I had done that too. I've slept in cars, spent endless hours sitting on park benches for lack of anywhere else to go, and have walked the streets of New York City, hoping to find enough loose change to buy a pack of cigarettes. I do not share these stories to gain your sympathy, for it was all a result of my own doing. I do not share this to be unique, for there are many people whose lives have experienced more pain than I can ever imagine. I share this with you, my friend, so that you will understand that, no matter where you are right now, you have within you the power to change your life, to take charge of your destiny, and to create the life you were born to live.

Today when I awaken each morning, before I get out of bed, I say a short prayer that I learned from the Reverend Robert Schuller, "This is the day which the Lord hath made. We will rejoice and be glad in it." For I know today that my life is a gift, and no matter what happens I am living a life beyond my wildest dreams.

My life today is magical. I have a loving wife, abundant health, and a wonderful home in one of the most beautiful parts of the United States. I am surrounded by nature, I have all the material possessions that I could possibly want; but more importantly, my life has purpose. I am privileged to spend my time speaking, writing, and being able to share what I have learned with others.

My books have been sold throughout the world, and I am fortunate to have been able to touch the lives of many, many people in a positive way. I get to speak to groups of people and share my message ,so that others may use these ideas in their own lives. The biggest thrill for me today is seeing the sparkle in a person's eye when they too realize that they can in fact create the life that they were born to live.

While I cannot see you at this time, I know that as you read this book and do the activities in it you will reach that point when your eyes sparkle, for you will have connected with the ideas presented here and will make them your own.

This is my intention, for I know we are all connected and that by sharing what we know with each other we will all benefit.

Remember the words of the English poet, John Donne (1573–1631), "No man is an island entire of itself; every man is a part of a continent, a part of the main."

1 N

Getting Started

> *"The significant problems we*
> *face cannot be solved at the*
> *same level of thinking we were*
> *at when we created them."*
>
> —ALBERT EINSTEIN

A good way to begin any personal growth program is by taking a close look at your life and all its components. If you were buying a business, the first thing you would do is access its current state of affairs. You would take inventory and examine the merchandise to determine what to keep and what to discard. You would examine the assets and take a look at the liabilities in order to know what to change.

We will do the same with our lives. Below I have listed various components that make up our lives. It is important to view your life in its entirety. To live a full and happy life requires balance in several areas. One of the challenges in our busy world today is maintaining that balance. Our tendency is to become focused on one area, like money or career, and neglect others such as our health or relationships. This can be devastating. You don't want to wind up with a lot of money at the expense of your family or health, do you? On the other hand, you don't want to be in great health but broke and homeless, without anyone who cares for you. It is important when doing personal growth work to maintain that delicate balance and devote time and attention to each of the key areas.

Activity

Following are the areas you will want to include in your inventory. For each of these areas, closely examine your life at the present time. Where are your strengths? What areas could use some improvement immediately? Choose one or two and set some immediate goals to begin work in those areas. Later, you will complete a goal-setting exercise that will incorporate each of these key areas.

- Spiritual

- Self-development

- Health and fitness

- Family, friends, and social relationships

- Career and business

- Social and material goals

- Money and investments

Thoughts Are Things

You may have heard the saying, "Thoughts are things." You've probably nodded your head in agreement, understanding that thoughts are, in fact, things. You probably believe this and accept that your thoughts, being things, do in fact have power.

Do you apply this to your day-to-day life? Have you stopped to consider the impact this has on your life experience?

Your thoughts produce emotions. Emotions, in turn, determine how you feel about a particular event or circumstance in your life. It has always amazed me how people can walk around feeling a particular way and not understand that it is their own thoughts, or more accurately what they are telling themselves, that is producing the feeling in the first place. This is why two people can look at the exact same thing and have opposite feelings about it.

You are creating your own reality, moment by moment, with the thoughts you think and what you say, both to yourself and others.

Let's explore this a little further. Most people will agree, and science can demonstrate, that everything in our world is a field of energy and has a particular frequency. The chair you're sitting on, your car, your cat, dog, your body, and everything else, including thoughts, has a field of energy or vibration. Recent scientific studies have identified particular ranges of frequencies and scientists are able to measure them.

Interestingly enough, negative energies like anger and rage measure very low on the scale, while positive energies like love and prayer reach the highest measurements. You can learn more about this work in *Power Versus Force* by David Hawkins, *The Messages of Water* by Masaru Emoto, and *Infinite Mind* by Dr. Valerie Hunt

The second part of this equation is the universal law that states "like attracts like." This has been referred to as the law of attraction, law of similars, and other names. What we choose to call it is not terribly important; what is important is understanding the part this plays in our lives.

Connecting the Dots

Let's supposing for a moment you're in a bad mood. You're feeling pretty negative. At that particular moment your personal vibration, the energy of your thoughts and words, is a low frequency. Let's call this particular mood, "frequency X."

Now somewhere off in the distant universe, there is another negative experience. Maybe it's a flat tire whose frequency happens to be "X" as well. By virtue of the law of attraction, you will begin attracting that or some other undesirable experience to you.

There are no accidents. The universe works on a specific set of principles that do not waiver. Like attracts like, whether we believe it or not.

The good news is that the opposite is also true. If, for example, you are feeling great—having invested time reading your goals and taking care to monitor your thoughts, intentions, and internal and external dialog—you are now entering a high energy vibration and are in a place to attract other high vibrations. These are generally the things you want to have in your life.

I'm not asking you to accept this blindly, only that you begin to observe the world around you and see if this holds true for you. I'm sure you've noticed situations when, in a room full of people, one person seems to be the center of attention. Why do you suppose this is? I'll give you a hint that's it's probably not her perfume.

Similarly, you probably know people who are always having undesirable experiences in their lives. These are the people who have a lousy time in even the best restaurant. They seem to travel with dark clouds over them and always experience things going wrong in their everyday lives. If you observe and listen to them closely, you will begin to see the connection between what they think and say and what shows up in their lives.

Activity: Watch Your Thoughts

Your exercise for the next week is to closely monitor your every thought and word. When you catch yourself dwelling in the negative, do something to interrupt your pattern and substitute a positive thought in its place. It has been said that any thought consistently held for about 15 to 20 seconds will begin to attract a similar energy. This is one of the reasons you want to read your life's vision and goals daily. This will hold your attention on thoughts of that which you want and help you manifest it.

2

Take Charge of Your Self-Talk

"Everything you do, everything you think, and everything you say is reflected back to you as your own experience."
—BUDDHIST TEACHING

It is impossible for a person to act or behave in a manner that is inconsistent with how he or she sees themselves. It is equally impossible for you to be in a resourceful state, demonstrating your best and highest capabilities, if you are consistently putting yourself down or, worse yet, allowing other people to belittle you.

What you tell yourself over and over is one of the major determinants to success in any given area of your life. What you listen to from other people is another key influencer of your behavior. Both of these, self-talk and talk from others, mold us and drive our behavior in any given situation.

What Do You Say to Yourself?

First, let's examine our self-talk more closely. Throughout out the day, during every waking hour, we are carrying on a running dialogue with ourselves. We are thinking or, more accurately, talking to ourselves constantly. Hundreds of words per minute pass through our conscious minds as we go about our day. Unfortunately, for one reason or another, most people's self-talk is negative. This is probably due to the number of negative messages we heard as we were growing up.

This came from other, perhaps well-intentioned, people or individuals who were themselves living in a negative reality. Much of it is from a steady stream of negativity bombarding us from television, radio, newspapers, and magazines. Situational comedies for the most part belittle people in the name of humor, and many game and reality shows place people in embarrassing situations, further undermining their self-image.

When you make a mistake, how do you respond? What do you say to yourself when you have trouble figuring out a computer program, for example? I have heard people tell themselves how stupid they are and how they never do anything right simply because they had trouble with a new software program. This is not only absurd and not true, it is quite damaging to your self-esteem.

What are you telling yourself? When you make a mistake do you view it as just that, a mistake? Learn from it and make a point not to repeat it? Or do you start belittling yourself with a stream of negative self-talk? Do you recognize, as Billy Joel wrote in one of his songs, "You're only human" and lighten up on yourself?

One of the reasons I have been able to learn new things easily is because, growing up, my mother would tell me how smart I was. Being a young child, I believed this and began to behave in a manner consistent with her opinion. While in my teenage years, I was a poor student and didn't like school, feeling it was too structured, still I've always found it easy to learn new things. When I reached an age where I saw the value of learning, I did so with ease. In television electronics school in the military, I finished second in my class.

To this day, I have a belief that learning is fun and easy, and I reinforce that belief with my self-talk. This serves me well especially in our rapidly changing technological world. I take to new ideas and technology like a fish takes to water.

We behave and perform in a manner that is consistent with what we believe about ourselves. Our beliefs are molded by what we tell ourselves over and over again. When you do something well, recognize it and reinforce the positive behavior with positive self-talk. When you make a mistake, see that it is just that, a mistake, and, realizing you are only human, tell yourself you'll do better next time. Use the power of your self-talk to help develop the habits and characteristics you want to create.

For example, when I am running on the treadmill at my health club, I repeat an affirmation I learned from Dr. Deepak Chopra: "Every day in every way I am increasing my mental and physical capacity." I consistently reinforce my exercise with positive self-talk, noticing my progress and telling myself how great I feel.

Author and speaker Brian Tracy suggests that people in sales repeat the phrase, "I'm a great sales person!" over and over for a few minutes prior to making a sales call. This conditions your mind for success and helps support a healthy self-image.

I frequently speak to groups who are at the lower end of the socio-economic scale and are struggling to improve their lives. I do this because, having been in that situation, I am able to connect with these people. When they realize I have been at the bottom too and have changed my life, they see it is possible for them to do the same thing. I am able to get my message across and I personally get a lot of satisfaction seeing a person believe they can change and begin seeing themselves differently.

What I've noticed among these groups of people is that their self-talk along with their self-image tends to be quite negative. They are quick to put themselves down and are very hard on themselves for even the slightest thing. Much of this is the result of the environment from which they came. I'll never forget one woman who, during a group workshop, asked me what I would do if everyone around me was always putting me down and belittling me. I replied simply, "I'd get away from them." These are the people my colleague Jack Canfield refers to as "toxic people." They are poisonous to your well-being.

These are the people in your life, sometimes people quite close to you, who keep trying to make you feel less than you are. For whatever reason— either they don't know any better or they believe that this is the way to motivate people. It's not! Perhaps they just want to make sure that you don't succeed and leave them behind.

Whatever their reasons, it is important for you to either get away from them or, at least, learn to ignore what they tell you. If someone close to you is telling you that you are stupid and will never get ahead, you can be saying to yourself, "You're wrong; I'm already getting ahead and becoming more successful each day," or something like that. Often we hear these negative messages at a very young age and carry them with us throughout our lives, replaying them over and over again.

I can still hear my grandfather's voice from when I was an adolescent, telling me I was a lazy bum just like my father and I would never amount to anything. I believe he loved me and that this was his way of getting me to change what were becoming some very poor habits and life choices. However, it did not work. All this did was undermine my already fragile self-esteem and make me feel worthless. I carried that message and replayed it in my own head for many years before I learned a better way.

We don't even realize the devastating impact such harsh words and criticism can have on a young person's mind. Children believe what they are told by the adults in their lives. One of the reasons we have such problems in our society with teenage alcohol and drug abuse is a lack of self-esteem. I know one thing with absolute certainty. If you have a healthy self-image, you do not need to abuse drugs or alcohol, commit crimes, or harm yourself or anyone else. One of the solutions to the problems that plague our society is to raise people's self-esteem.

Watch What You Say

"Now don't you go getting any ideas, Harold; don't you get any ideas either, Angie; don't you two get any ideas."

The young mother's words to her small children echoed in my head for several days. While I realized she was probably warning them to not do something against her wishes or something that could harm them, I can't help but wonder about the effects that a situation like that, heard over and over for a period of years, will have on their lives and their ability to realize their potential.

Flash forward—it's twenty years later and now little Harold and Angie are all grown up, sitting in a conference room where they both work as marketing managers, having graduated at the top of their classes in college. The CEO is pacing back and forth saying, "Okay gang, what we need now, if we want to save this company, are some really good ideas."

As their bosses words trail off, Harold and Angie are jolted back in time to that day at the Eagle Diner. All they can hear is their mother's voice telling them not to get any ideas. The conflict that this is causing has blocked their creative abilities. The contribution they might have made has been stifled by a poor choice of phrasing some twenty years ago.

I know this sounds a bit extreme, but if you stop and think about it this happens all the time. We are constantly being conditioned by the messages we hear, especially in our formative years.

We use phrases like "don't get smart" and then wonder why children are doing poorly in school. See the connection? Whatever is repeated over and over will be absorbed into the subconscious mind of the person listening—in this case your children. McDonald's knows this, as does every other successful advertiser.

My wife can still sing the toothpaste commercial she saw on television when she was eight years old, and every child in the developed world can sing McDonald's commercials. The words you choose and the phrases you use repeatedly will have a lasting impact on your children. Why not choose words that will help them realize their potential as unique, creative, bright, loving, powerful, and successful human beings?

Imagine what could happen if you made a habit of using positive, empowering, self-esteem building messages every day? Imagine all your children could become!

Decide right now to create some positive messages you can implant in the young minds of your children. Make a daily habit of using positive messages when speaking to your children.

For example, you might say, "You know, (child's name), every day you're getting better and better in every way." (This is a takeoff on a phrase from Claude Bristol's classic self-help book, *The Magic of Believing*.)

Put Away the Stick

Trying to change a person's behavior by mentally or emotionally berating them is like trying to fix a computer problem with a hammer. You would not even consider such an act, but we do this, without thinking, to the people in our lives.

Be careful what you say to others, especially children. Choose words that will encourage rather than berate them. We can all work a little harder to raise our self-esteem and that of everyone we encounter. One of the reasons that I am attracted to the coaching profession is because it is the aim of every professional coach to become our personal best and help others to do the same. By raising each other up we all benefit. It is possible to create a society in which everyone succeeds. We can create a win-win world.

A generation or two ago, many people believed that the way to improve someone's behavior was to mentally and emotionally abuse the person by belittling them and criticizing their actions. Unfortunately, there are some people who still believe this is an effective method. We know today that it is not. We know today that berating someone to try to improve their behavior, as I said before, is akin to hitting a computer with a hammer to make it perform better.

I remember coming home from grade school one day excited that I had received 85 percent on my report card in a particular subject, only to have my father ask, "Why didn't you get 95 percent?" Don't get me wrong, I'm not blaming him. He did what he thought was the best way to get me to improve. This was how he was raised, and he was just doing what he thought was the right thing to do.

We know today that a better approach would have been for him to say, "That's great Jim. How might you improve even more next marking period?" This would have contributed to raising my self-imagine and increase the likelihood of my performing better in the future.

Getting the Best out of People

In sales and business we still find companies whose sales managers will berate their sales people saying something like, "What's wrong with you? Are you totally incompetent? You only made three sales when you were supposed to make five." More effective sales managers know that the way to raise their people up is to first acknowledge their success and then coach them to set new goals to do even better. A more effective scenario might sound more like this, "John, you had three sales last week. That's great news. Now, let's look at how you did that and see how you might reach your goal of five sales next week." By recognizing their success, the effective sales managers reinforce the salesperson's self-esteem and set the stage to help them grow and improve in the future.

One of the most effective weight loss programs in the world, Weight Watchers International, cheers people who have achieved any amount of weight loss, even one quarter or one half a pound. While this may not seem important when the person wants to lose 50 or 60 pounds, it is critical to encourage them to continue to follow the program. This is one of the reasons why this program has been so successful for so many years.

By celebrating even the smallest weight loss, the individual's self-image improves. They begin to see themselves succeeding in the program, and it reinforces their commitment to continue. The small successes are what we need to achieve the big goal.

As I mentioned earlier, building people's self-esteem is something that is crucial for us to do more of in our society. If you want to learn more about this, I suggest that you contact the National Association for Self-Esteem (www.self-esteem-nase.org).

With teenage suicide and drug abuse at an all-time high, it is more important than ever to be helping our youth—and for that matter, everyone around us—to raise their self-esteem and feel better about who they are. The more we do this, the more we will improve our society.

Energy Vampires

In addition to the toxic people there is another group to avoid whenever possible. They are "energy vampires." You know the ones I mean. These are the people who leave you feeling emotionally drained after spending only four or five minutes talking with them. It's like they just suck the energy from you with all of their negativity and complaining. Because we are, in fact, affected by the energy around us, this is very real. If we stay in a negative situation for periods of time, we will be affected by the negativity there.

Energy vampires include those people who can't wait to tell you about the latest disaster which you can do nothing to change and which will only cause you to feel badly if you let it. They are also those people who spend endless hours telling you about their latest surgeries and intimate medical details as if telling you is going to help, when in fact all it does is drain more of your energy.

Stick with the Winners

I'm not suggesting that you be insensitive or unsympathetic to people who need someone to talk to, just that you minimize your interaction with those people, especially with those who do it constantly. You know who I'm talking about. There are people in all of our lives who, when we spend a little time with them, leave us feeling lousy, not even knowing why. It's because they literally suck the energy out of us. If you want to have a happier and more fulfilling life and be more successful, hang out with people who are positive and support your dreams.

One of the things that I learned when I first entered a program of recovery was to "stick with the winners." You stick close to those people who want to succeed at whatever they're doing and avoid the ones who want to live their lives complaining and sitting around moaning and groaning about their lot in life, doing nothing but depressing themselves and everyone around them.

Attitude Is Everything

If you call my friend and colleague Jeff Keller on the telephone, you are greeted by an uplifting, cheery voice who answers, "Attitude is everything." You see, besides being his main philosophy in life, it is the name of his company and the title of his first book. Jeff is one of the people whom I turn to when I'm feeling less than great for he is always helpful and encouraging. He has been a great friend for many years and his message reminds all of us of the importance of our attitude in shaping who we become and what we accomplish in our lives.

A negative attitude not only makes a person unpleasant to be around but robs them of their potential. Whenever we allow ourselves to slip into a negative attitude we take away our potential for problem solving. It is virtually impossible to be in a creative, resourceful state while in a negative state of mind. We literally do not have access to the power within us when we are negative. We shut off any possibility to succeed.

A Wonderful Person but Hard to Be Around

My mother-in-law, rest her soul, had a habit of looking at a situation or something on the news and saying, "I feel so bad about _____." I doubt it is a coincidence that she spent the better part of her life unhappy and when asked how she felt never replied "terrific." Be careful what you speak, think, or say to yourself and others. Remember your subconscious mind, that part of your mind that is just beneath your waking state, does not know the difference between real and imaginary. If you continually say, "I feel bad," you begin to feel bad. Like attracts like; it is a universal law. On the other hand, if you want to feel good most of the time, focus on the things that make you feel good. Tell yourself things that leave you feeling good. Use powerful questions like, "What am I happy about?" or "What is the best thing that happened to me today?" to cause you to feel even better.

3

Take Charge of Your Beliefs

"The greatest discovery is that a human being can alter his life by altering his attitudes of mind."
—**WILLIAM JAMES**

*B*eliefs are one of my favorite subjects. If there is one thing that keeps people from having everything they want in their lives, it is what they believe about themselves, their abilities, and the world in which they live. Everything that you do in your life and everything that you have accomplished or will ever accomplish is directly governed by your beliefs.

Where Do Beliefs Come From?

A belief, quite simply, is a thought that you have held or something that you have told yourself over and over throughout your life. Beliefs start at a young age. If we try something for the first time and we fail, we label ourselves a failure. For example, if at the age of 10 or 12 I attempted to play basketball but because of my age and size was not very good at it, I may have created a belief in my own mind that I cannot play basketball. This may not have been true, because beliefs rarely are.

A more common example is the person who once tried their own business but was not successful. They created a belief that they are not meant to be in business and therefore never tried it again. This is really sad when you consider that almost every successful business person has experienced many "failures." The difference is in the way they viewed the experience and the beliefs that they created from them. One person may see a business "failure" as a sign they cannot be a successful business owner, while the other will only view it as a temporary setback and turn it into a learning experience.

Other People's Beliefs

Perhaps the most limiting and destructive beliefs are those we are given by other people and society in general. There is something called a "global belief" which is what happens when a whole section of society agrees that something is true.

Many of the long held, global beliefs that were later proven to be false are things like "Man was not meant to fly." In the case of Roger Banister the first human being to run a mile in less than four minutes it was, "Man cannot run a mile in under four minutes." That particular belief was in place for thousands of years before Mr. Banister came along and shattered it. Many times a child is told, "You can't do that, you're too small," and, believing the adult, the child carries this belief with them throughout their lives. They begin to apply it to everything that is a challenge, "I can't do that, I'm too small," and see themselves as being too small in this world.

One of my favorite belief stories happened to me several years ago when I started a publication for small business owners. I had an idea that there was a need for a local publication that would give the small business owner information to help them in their businesses, and I decided to do it.

Quite honestly, I did not have a lot of knowledge or experience in publishing a magazine, but I knew enough to get started and I trusted my instincts so I went ahead with it. I had placed an ad in our local newspaper for a sales person to help with selling the advertising and interviewed several people.

The day after the first issue was published, one of the people I interviewed called me. He was an advertising sales person for a weekly newspaper and, while he wished me well, had decided not to change jobs. We had spoken in early June, and it was now the first week of September. The premier issue was out in time for Labor Day, as I had promised the advertisers.

The man called and asked, "How did you do it?" I replied, "How did I do what?" He said, "How did you publish this magazine so quickly? It was only two months ago and you were just getting started." I thought for a moment and told the man the truth—I had no idea how long it was supposed to take to publish a magazine. I had no beliefs about the time needed. He told me that it takes at least six months to bring out a new publication. That was not a fact. It was merely his belief. Because of my inexperience I had no such belief and published the magazine within three months.

How Your Beliefs Determine Your Results

Let's take a closer look at exactly how our beliefs determine results. Most people would agree that we have unlimited potential. Why then do we not see this in the results that we produce? This is where beliefs come into play. The result you produce is determined by the actions you take. The problem is, most of us have a limiting belief in our ability to accomplish a particular task. We only tap into a small portion of our potential, take limited action, and produce a poor result.

An example of this principal is the dieter who tries eating healthier for a few days but then gives up because they believe they cannot successfully lose weight, or the salesperson who makes a few calls before deciding that this is not for them and moves on to yet another business. In reality, it was their limiting belief in their own ability that caused them to take such little action in the first place.

Fortunately, the opposite is also true. If you develop a belief you can do whatever you set your mind to, you will tap into more of your limitless potential, take massive amounts of action, and produce even greater results.

My favorite example of this principal is the story of one of my mentors and favorite people, Jack Canfield, the coauthor of the *Chicken Soup for the Soul* series. Jack and his co-author Mark Victor Hansen were turned down more than 140 times when they were first trying to get their book published. Because of their strong beliefs in themselves and their book, they continued, talking to publisher after publisher, until finally at the American Booksellers Association conference, a relatively unknown publisher decided to take a chance and publish the book.

Chicken Soup for the Soul has gone on to break all records for non-fiction books, has evolved into numerous spinoff books, and more than seventy other products have been licensed from it.

All of this was possible because of the strongly held belief that Jack and Mark had about their ability to succeed and a deeply held belief in the value of their wonderful book. It was their beliefs that caused them to continue to take massive action and not give up. When asked what they would have done had their publisher not agreed to publish the book, they said they would have kept on asking.

My Early Sales Experience

Many years ago I worked as a door-to-door salesperson selling vacuum cleaners. I was eighteen years old, it was my first real sales job, and I had a lot of fun doing it. I actually took the job on a dare. The manager told me I was too young to be a salesman and I replied, with just a bit of youthful arrogance, "I will be your top salesman within my first month."

He accepted my challenge and hired me. I would be out working in my territory early in the day, eagerly ringing doorbells, and more often than not would have a sale by early afternoon.

This was above average, so for quite a few days I would knock off early and head to the office to turn in my paperwork, planning to call it a day and go home. Walter, my manager, knowing I was planning on going home early, devised a way to keep me working.

Actually, it was years later when I realized what he was doing. When I came into the office, he would take me aside and ask me to do him a favor. He would point to a section on the map and tell me that he had canvassed there just a few weeks earlier and that there was a woman who wanted to buy a new vacuum cleaner. He told me he did not remember exactly which house it was, but if I would just canvass (ring doorbells) for a few blocks in either direction near a particular street I would be sure to find her.

Believing this would be an easy sale, I would take the bait. I would go out and begin walking the streets he suggested, and every single time I would find the house where he said the woman wanted to buy a new vacuum cleaner.

It would be many years before I thought about that experience and realized that there was no such woman. He had not worked in the area and made the whole thing up to keep me working and to keep me from going home early.

The interesting thing was that because I believed Walter, I would sell a unit each and every time. My belief that there was a customer ready to buy was all it took for me to find a sale.

We will consistently perform in accordance with what we believe about ourselves, our capabilities, and the world we live in. This is why it is so important, so crucial, to create beliefs that will empower us and help us become the people we know we are capable of becoming.

The Courage to Change

It's not always easy to change. Often it means doing new things and letting go of beliefs you may have held for most of your life. If you really want to live the life you deserve, it's essential to let go of those beliefs that are not supporting you. We've all said at one time or another, "That's just the way I am." This is like the severely overweight person who says, "I have big bones." This is nonsense! Anyone can change their beliefs about themselves, and in the next few pages we will explore ways to do just that.

Removing the Illusion

Any belief that you have about yourself is the result of a combination of several things. It is something that you have told yourself over and over again or others have told you over and over again until you believe it to be true. The driving forces behind our beliefs, and perhaps the strongest determinators, are the references that we have created to support a given belief. For example, if a person has gone on a diet and not lost more than a few pounds, very often they will create a belief of "not being able to lose weight." Their failed attempt becomes the reference that supports their belief. They say things like, "See, I tried, but I just can't do it."

I once spoke with a woman who had written a children's book. When I asked her about having it published she told me she had tried but no publisher wanted to take it on. This, by the way, was merely a belief.

I questioned her about having submitted the book to children's book publishers, and she had in fact done so. I asked, "How many?" She replied, "Three." She had sent her book to a mere three publishers, and when they declined she created a belief that no one wanted to publish her book and gave up. In contrast, as I said before, the authors of *Chicken Soup for the Soul* presented their manuscript to more than 140 publishers before finding one that agreed to publish it.

One way to begin to shift your limiting beliefs is to question the references that are supporting them and replace them with new ones that will empower you to create what you want. References are like the legs on a stool—they support the belief. If you begin to break down the references, you weaken the belief in the same way that you would weaken the stool if you began to break the legs.

In the case of the woman with the children's book, all she had to do was realize that, although three publishers turned her down, there are more than 50,000 publishers in the United States alone. It would have been obvious that a belief of "no one wants to publish my book" was pure nonsense. The truth of the matter was that she was not committed enough to keep going. She could have created a belief like, "There are plenty of publishers left. I'm sure one will want my book."

Let's begin now to shift some of your limiting beliefs.

Moving Through the Gap

There is always a gap between your present circumstance and the one you want to experience. It's human nature to want to expand and grow. It's perfectly natural to want to experience more while at the same time being happy and grateful for all we've already received in our lives.

Who among us does not want more love, vibrant health, a more fulfilling relationship with our loved ones, more challenging work, more creativity, and, yes, more money? If it were not for people wanting more material possessions, most of the great companies in the world would not exist and much of the world's population would not have jobs.

If people like Bill Gates (Microsoft), Akio Morita (Sony), Sakichi Toyota (Toyota), Coco Chanel (Chanel), or Mary Kay Ash (Mary Kay) were satisfied with creating just enough for themselves, the thousands of people who work for their companies would be unemployed. The people who believe it is somehow incorrect or greedy to want more simply do not understand the world in which we live.

Of course there are greedy people, but fortunately they usually fail sooner or later. We have all seen these people in the recent news stories about how their unscrupulous actions led to the downfall of several large corporations. Most of them are now serving time in jails as a result of their greed. In my opinion, this is a good place for them to reflect on their behavior.

When I refer to wanting more, I'm referring to people like you and I who want to create more, not only to help ourselves and our loved ones but, hopefully, to have a positive impact on society as well. It is possible for the entire population of the world to live in abundance. The only limits in our world are those imposed by ourselves. God's universe knows no lack. If you doubt this, go out and count the number of seeds in a tomato and realize that each is capable of producing an entire plant which will bring many, many more tomatoes. Try to count the blades of grass in a lawn or the trees in a forest. The only lack in our world is a result of our own thinking.

To get back to the original point, the only difference between where you are right now and having what you want is the belief. For example, I believe I drive a new car. I believe it because it is in my driveway. This was not always the case. There was a time years ago when I was without a car and walked or took the bus everywhere. There was a time after that when I drove an old car that would break down on a regular basis. I used to leave it parked and sometimes forget to take the keys out of the ignition. This wasn't a problem because it was not the kind of car anyone would steal. What it took for me to attract a new car into my life was to begin to believe I could have it and to do the work that would make it possible for me to afford it.

Overcoming Resistance

Where a lot of people have problems with setting and achieving goals is that the gap between where they are and where they want to be is so huge their mind cannot believe it is possible to have what they want. Sure, writing goals and repeating affirmations about what you want will eventually bring it to you, but more often than not, people give up before they reach their goals because their internal belief is so strong that it overrides their desire.

Crossing the Chasm

So how do we get past this? I use a technique called, a "bridge belief." It's really quite simple. Consider your current reality as a starting point. For example, "I have no money," is a belief shared by many people.

Of course, when most people say they have "no money," they really mean they have just enough to get by with their living expenses. I've been in situations when I literally had "no money," and believe me it is a very different situation.

I've always liked what theater producer and showman Mike Todd said when a reporter asked him what it was like to be poor. Todd replied, "I have never been poor, I've been broke. Poor is a state of mind; broke is a temporary condition."

Let's suppose your goal is "financial independence." In order to have financial independence you would need to believe that you have lots of money. Can you see the huge gap between these two realities? On one side of the gap, "I have no money," and on the other side of the gap, "I have lots of money." Trying to shift from a belief of "I have no money" to a belief of "I have lots of money" is like trying to jump the Snake River Canyon on a motorcycle. This is something that was attempted by daredevil Evel Knievel, who was seriously hurt attempting it.

A more effective method of achieving what you want and creating a new reality is to gradually move toward it by shifting your beliefs a little at a time. For example, a new belief you could use to move from "I have no money" might be, "I have just begun a part-time business that will increase my income."

While this is not the desired outcome of "I have lots of money," it is further along than the original, low-energy belief and will begin to move you in the direction of your dreams. As your "current reality" begins to shift, you can create another bridge belief that is even closer to your desired outcome until, one day, your desire and your reality are the same and you have whatever it is you want. By using the bridge belief, you will begin feeling better and be moving toward what you want.

Your Bridge Belief

Think about one thing that you really, really want to change. Perhaps it's your weight. What is your current reality? Is it, "I'm overweight and out of shape"? What is your desired reality? Is it, "I look and feel great and I am healthy and fit"? This is obviously a long way from where you are now.

You could work with a new affirmation like "I'm exercising, eating better, and becoming healthier each day." While this may not be all the way to your goal, it will make you feel better than your current belief. The better you begin to feel about yourself, the more motivated you will be to achieve your goal.

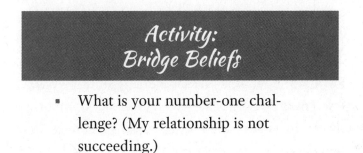

Activity:
Bridge Beliefs

- What is your number-one challenge? (My relationship is not succeeding.)

- What is your present belief? (I can't go on with this.)

- What is your desired reality? (I have a happy and loving relationship.)

- Create your bridge belief. (My partner and I are finding new ways to appreciate each other.)

By affirming your new bridge belief, which you now believe because it is true, you'll begin feeling better. This new feeling will help you move toward to your desired goals. As you progress, you will change your bridge belief to match your new, improved reality until, one day, it will match what you want and you will have it.

A Powerful, Life-changing Question

Do you find yourself saying things like "If only I had such and such, then I would be happy"? Do you have a dream that is really burning inside you but think you'll never achieve it because of some insurmountable obstacle? Did you create the obstacle in your mind, or did someone else put it there?

In my coaching practice I consistently notice these walls standing between people and their dreams. Interestingly enough, the wall is usually in the person's own mind and not really the obstacle that they think it is. Very often it's not even theirs but was put there by some well-intentioned friend or family member. Once we remove the wall, the person is on their way to living their dreams.

Taking Down the Walls

One way that you can begin to remove your walls or blocks is to use a powerful question. Powerful questions are used by coaches to help people move through whatever is blocking them.

For example, you could ask yourself something like, "How could I accomplish what I want with the resources I presently have?" This simple yet powerful question changed my life.

Years ago I had an idea for a video program. The problem was I did not have the necessary resources to produce a video. At that time broadcast quality video production was quite expensive. I spent several years with my idea sitting dormant, deluding myself that "someday I'll be able to produce it." One day, which happened to be my birthday, I was listening to a tape that suggested that I use the above question to shift my thinking and take down the wall I had built.

When I applied the question "What resources do I presently have?" to my idea of producing a video, I realized that while I was not in position to produce the video, I did have the resources necessary to write and produce a book.

That day I began writing my first book, *Handbook to a Happier Life* (New World Library). My life has never been the same since.

Changing to a more empowering question lead me to a totally new sense of purpose. I have since written and published several books, which have been translated into numerous languages and are sold throughout the world. All this is the result of asking a different, more empowering question.

So often we erect these huge walls that limit our progress and keep us from our dreams. By using a different question you can uncover alternative methods to accomplish your goal. By using a different question you can become unstuck and move toward what you desire.

Alisha's Story

A client of mine had a dream to build a healing and counseling center. Looking at her business plan, I noticed a huge wall standing in her way. The plan called for almost a million dollars in startup capital. When I asked her why she needed so much money, she replied, "To buy the building." I could easily see this was not essential. I asked her if and how she could begin right now with what she had, without the building. I saw a sparkle in her eyes as she realized that it was possible to begin her business right then and there, with the resources she had. Her original business plan is still intact; however, she is now moving in the direction of her dream.

The building was not the business or the dream. The dream was to help people, and once we uncovered that the building became unnecessary. It was merely a wall that stood between her and her passion. With the wall removed, she is free to pursue a lifelong dream of helping people heal. I am certain that one day she will have her building; but in the meantime, she is doing what she loves.

Activity:
Take Down the Walls

If you want to move toward creating the life of your dreams, complete the following exercise:

- What walls have you or someone else erected?

- How else might you accomplish your objective using the resources you already have?
- How could you begin right now?
- Who can help?

4

Take Charge of Your Emotions

"The more you praise and celebrate your life, the more there is in life to celebrate."

—OPRAH WINFREY

*I*n order for you to live a happy and productive life and to really take charge of your destiny, it is necessary for you to take control of your emotional states rather than letting them control you. As I have said before, your emotions are a result of thinking a particular thought. A thought will trigger a series of similar thoughts and internal dialog that will cause the emotional state. The states that I'm referring to here and the ones that you will want to take control of are those undesirable states like rage, anger, overwhelm, fear, helplessness, and other emotional states that you may experience regularly and that are blocking your progress.

Motion Equals Emotion

The fastest way I know of to change an unwanted emotional state is to start moving. That's right, move! The next time you're feeling down or depressed, get up and go for a walk. Of course, I'm not referring to clinical depression. If you suffer from constant depression, please seek professional help. I'm talking about those moods we all experience from time to time. By changing your physiology, you will change your emotional state. This is one reason that people usually feel happier after rigorous exercise. Just taking a brisk walk, run, or swim will help you to feel better and increase your mental capacity and creativity. I have found that if I am feeling down and I take a twenty- or thirty-minute walk, I feel better. Physical movement will always have a positive effect on your emotional state.

In order to take charge of an emotional state, you will need to begin to identify its cause or trigger. Prior to experiencing any emotional state, something happens in our minds. We think a thought, which then acts as a trigger for the state to be born. One thought leads to another in rapid succession until, before we even realize it, we are in the undesirable state.

Suppose you are driving down the highway, peacefully going about your business, when all of a sudden out of nowhere someone cuts right in front of you, almost taking off your bumper. Has this ever happened to you? I'm guessing it has, and I'm also guessing that it changed your otherwise peaceful mood radically and instantly. Typically, when this happens, we think something like, "What a fool. How can he cut me off like that?" This leads to a series of similar thoughts until our mood is totally disrupted. If we let the thoughts continue we will have produced the state known as "road rage." While road rage is nothing more than an extreme reaction to an event that has occurred on a road or highway, it has caused serious problems, even death, for those who allowed themselves to be overcome by it. The entire episode of road rage could have been eliminated if the person chose a different thought in the first place; however, this is easier said than done.

In the heat of the moment, it may be difficult to think rationally. In these situations we can shift our focus and look at it in a different way. This will break the pattern long enough for us to shift to a more rational thought. For example, in our driving situation when the person cut in front of our car, instead of going into a tirade, we could marvel how the person did that with total disregard for anyone around him. You could shift your thinking to asking yourself what prompted someone to do such a dangerous and foolish thing. Perhaps she was rushing to the hospital to see her child who was just injured in an accident, or he was summoned to the bedside of his dying mother and wanted to get there in time. Imagining these scenarios, which shift our feelings from anger to compassion, will eliminate rage and keep us calm regardless of what was going on around us.

Anchoring Yourself with Music

Music is a powerful emotional anchor that you can use to recreate a desirable emotional or mental state. There are times when I am going to speak to a group and I'm not feeling at my peak energy level. The group listening to me, however, deserves me at my very best, so I have developed several rituals to help raise my energy. One of the most powerful ones is music. I keep some very specific music in a playlist on my phone to play while I am on my way there. One song in particular that instantly puts me in a peak state is Billy Joel's "We Didn't Start the Fire."

This song was played at the Fire Walk Seminar that I participated in many years ago. It was where I confronted my fears by walking barefoot over a bed of hot coals. Whenever I hear that song I immediately connect with the intense energy and peak emotion that I experienced that night as I was preparing to walk over the coals. It was a life-altering experience to say the least. Playing that song immediately changes my energy level regardless of how I may be feeling at the time.

If you were to come home from work totally exhausted and wanted to do nothing more than sit and watch TV and I walked in and handed you $50,000 to go out and buy whatever you wanted, provided you went out right away, do you think you would muster the energy to do it? Of course you would. You would immediately forget that you were tired and jump up ready to go.

Rarely are we actually as tired as we think. More often than not, our feeling tired is a mental drain, not a physical state, and can be quickly altered by changing our emotional state. Of course, there are times when we are really exhausted and need to rest.

If you want to easily recreate a pleasant emotional state, keep some music around that has special meaning to you and will make you feel good. The song "I Got You (I Feel Good)" by James

Brown is one that will have a positive effect on almost everyone. Another song that tends to do the same thing is "Celebration" by Kool and the Gang, from the late 1970s.

Pattern Interrupt: Fear of Calling

Sometimes you can use a technique known as a "pattern interrupt." This is merely an action that causes you to break your thought pattern long enough to substitute a new thought. It comes from the science of Neuro Linguistic Programming (NLP) developed by Richard Bandler and John Grindler.

Let's say you have a fear of making cold calls on the telephone. After all, calling strangers can be intimidating, and this fear is quite prevalent in most sales jobs. Before the fear sets in, when you are about to make your call, devise a technique which will interrupt your pattern and break the fear thought long enough for you to simply grab the phone and dial the number.

You may do something like jump up and down and yell "yes" or raise your arms in the air over your head, kind of like the boxing champions do when they win a bout. Any physical action will usually interrupt your thought pattern long enough for you to begin the action. Once you begin, the fear usually subsides.

Another area where you might use this technique is if you have a tendency to eat a less-than-healthy diet. Your desire for the food or craving usually starts with a thought, which leads to another thought and so on. These thoughts build in intensity until you have created a first-class craving for a particular food or taste. By the time you have reached that point, the craving is in control and you will most likely eat the unhealthy food. By developing ahead of time a specific pattern interrupt, you will have something you can use to catch yourself before the random thought becomes a craving. You could have a thought about eating a big piece of chocolate cake. Left alone this thought will begin to trigger other thoughts about how good this would taste and how much you want it until it is a craving and you have literally lost control of the situation.

Instead of trying to think yourself out of the situation, something that is possible but quite difficult, you can eliminate the craving more easily by using your predetermined pattern interrupt. When you have the first thought you could stand, take several breaths, drink a big glass of water, or go for a brief walk. You might use a "special phrase" like the one my wife uses to help keep her health on track. When Georgia wants to avoid eating something, she says to herself, "Nothing tastes as good as thin feels." Sooner than you realize, you will forget about wanting the cake.

Any of these would break the thought pattern and, most likely, the thought or desire will have passed. Remember you can only think one thought at a time. You can use this same technique in your relationships with your spouse, family, or coworkers. For example, you and your spouse could agree that, at the start of an argument, before either party goes into their arguing ritual, you will simply hold each other's hands. It's surprising how it is almost impossible to have a heated argument while holding the other person's hand. The intensity of hand holding connects us at a much deeper level and the anger tends to dissipate. The next time you feel yourself and your spouse are about to get into a heated discussion, take the other persons hand in yours and take a few deep breaths. You will find yourselves becoming calmer and feel more connected to each other. This makes it much more likely you will find an amicable solution to your difference of opinion.

Change Your Life

My colleague Vinny Roazzi, the author of *The Spirituality of Success*, is fond of saying, "If you want to change your life, you have to change your life." What this means is that if you want to make changes and experience your life at a different level, you must be willing to change. Once you begin to change your beliefs about what is possible for your life, you must be willing to do whatever it takes. This usually requires you to change some of your habits and activities.

When my life began to turn around after hitting my lowest point, it became clear to me that I would have to make significant changes if I was to have the kind of life I wanted.

The path I was on was going nowhere but down, and if I did not change I would probably die—or worse, continue to live in the hell that my life had become. I was in so much spiritual, mental, physical, and emotional pain that I would have done anything to change my life.

I changed my habits, I changed where I lived, my work, I even changed the kind of music I listened to. I went from "party animal" to becoming a quiet, reflective person. I traded late nights and crazy times for early mornings and solitude. I asked God to come back into my life and reconnected with my spiritual side. Having been a night owl, I changed my sleeping habits and learned to like getting up early in the morning, about the same time I used to come in from a night on the town.

I'm not suggesting that everyone do this or that there is anything wrong with partying, but this is what I had to do because the life I was leading was killing me.

All too often I hear people talking about how they want their lives to change. Some want a better relationship, to lose weight, start a business, or earn more money. However, they continue doing the same things they have always done. Nothing changes. It can't be both ways.

One definition of insanity is doing the same thing and expecting a different result. If you want to change your life, you must change your life. If you want to weigh less and be healthier, it is necessary to embark on a regular exercise program and make healthier food choices. Always begin by having a physical check-up and consultation with a health practitioner to help you establish a program.

If what you want is financial independence and security, you will need to change your relationship with money. You may need to learn more about finances and investments, change your spending habits, or some combination of both. You may want to begin your own part- or full-time business. We'll discuss finance in greater detail later in this book, but for now just realize that anything you want that you do not already have will require some form of change.

The person who wants a better relationship with their spouse or children might need to change the way they relate and communicate with them. The parent who wants a better relationship with their child, but is busy working, may want to reevaluate their priorities and make some changes in their schedule to allow more time for their children.

This is one of the main reasons so many people are starting their own businesses and working from home. Many parents, especially those with very young children, are finding that working from home gives them the extra time to devote to their children's upbringing and makes it easier to juggle a family and career.

What changes will you make? Do you spend your spare time surfing the Internet or watching television when what you really want is financial freedom? Doing that will not get you there. Perhaps trading a night of television to take a class in a new skill or subject will move you closer to your dream life. If you want to learn more about finance, business, or investments, there are plenty of evening programs you can enroll in which will teach you what you need to know. You can even find programs that you can take right on the Internet.

If you want to have better health, you could trade some of your "couch potato" time and go for a walk or enroll in an exercise program.

Activity

We will explore dreams, goals, plans, and how to achieve them later in this book. For now, simply list in your journal one immediate change that you will commit to making in each of the following key areas of your life.

- Spiritual

- Self-development

- Health and fitness

- Family, friends, and social relationships

- Career and business

- Social and material

- Money and investments

5

Take Charge of Your Dreams

"If you can dream it, begin it.
For our dreams have magic
and power in them."

—JOHANN WOLFGANG VON GOETHE

To dream is to live. To dream is to feel the excitement and possibilities the future holds for us.

Our dreams are what make us want to jump out of bed each morning eager to begin a new day. They are what propel us through life and give meaning to our existence. They are what makes the difference between a life fully lived with joy, passion, and fulfillment or one, as Henry David Thoreau said, "of quiet desperation."

You have dreams. You may have forgotten them or put them aside because you were told, "Stop dreaming and be realistic," but you have them nonetheless. By the way, by the time you have finished reading this book, I hope I have convinced you that neither of those beliefs serve your best interests. Never stop dreaming. Dreams are what have given us everything that we have in our society. A simple dream born in the heart and mind of an ordinary woman or man is what has given us every invention, every advance in technology, medicine, science, and the arts. Dreamers have given us virtually every advancement we have made since the dawn of civilization.

You too have a God-given birthright to see your dreams a reality. You have a right to live your dreams to the fullest and use them to create the life you were born to live.

What Happened to Our Dreams?

As young children we all had dreams about who we wanted to become and what we wanted to accomplish. As we grew older, we were taught by well-intentioned individuals to put our dreams aside and "be sensible." Our educational system, for the most part, has been designed to discourage independent thinking. It teaches everyone to walk to the beat of the same drummer. We were taught to draw "within the lines" and "follow the rules." It is interesting to note that most people who have achieved excellence in any field have done so by stepping out of the box. Many of our most accomplished citizens—people like Albert Einstein and Thomas Edison, holder of numerous patents and the inventor of the electric light bulb—were very poor students in school. Bill Gates, presently the wealthiest man in the world, dropped out of Harvard to pursue his passion for computers. I'm not suggesting that education is unnecessary, just don't let it get in the way of you walking to "the beat of your own drummer."

Education was put in perceptive for me many years ago. At the time, I was in business with a man named Irving Goldmacher, one of the two smartest people I have ever met. The other one, incidentally, is my wife Georgia. At age 24, Irving had achieved two Masters degrees, one in electrical engineering and the other in physics, was a senior engineer, and had received several patents for his designs for antenna guidance systems.

I, on the other hand, often felt inferior to people because I barely finished high school, until one day Irving said to me, "James (he called me James),

I am thankful that my formal education did not screw up my ability to think." How profound! I told you he was smart.

Never give up your dreams; never let anyone talk you out of a dream that is important to you. If not for the dreamers, this world would be a pretty dull place. Dreamers and visionaries accomplish great feats even though they don't always know exactly how they will do it at the time. President John F. Kennedy had a dream in 1960 to put a man on the moon by the end of the decade, and in July of 1969 Neil Armstrong became the first man to walk on the face of the moon. It's interesting to note that at the time he set the goal, neither he nor NASA knew exactly how they were going to accomplish it. This is an important point about goal-setting. You need not be concerned with how you will accomplish what you want until later in the process. First, you must know what you want.

You're Never Too Old

Often in seminars someone will say to me "I'm too old" to change or to realize my dreams. This is pure nonsense. As long as you have a pulse, you can move toward realizing your dreams. Of course there are some exceptions. If you're 75 and want to be a professional baseball player, this is not likely to happen; however, there are lots of other dreams you can fulfill regardless of your age. For example, Ray Kroc founded McDonald's at age 54 and at 65 Harlan (Colonel) Sanders began KFC. On July 24, 1987, Hulda Crooks became the oldest person to climb Mt. Fuji in Japan. She was 91 at the time. Upon doing so, she exclaimed, "You always feel good when you make a goal." I've always enjoyed the story about the woman who told author and motivational speaker Wally Amos that at fifty-four, if she were to go to law school, in three years when she graduated she would be fifty-seven. Wally asked her how old she would be in three years if she did not go to law school.

Several years ago, my local newspaper published a story about a man who had worked in a dry cleaning store for 21 years without missing a day of work. What made the story unique was that the man was 81 years old when he was hired! The man, then 103 years old, was still going strong.

What are some of your dreams? What is it that you would like to have in your life? What would you like to do? Where would you like to go? Who would you like to meet? What would you like to be known for? What would you like to leave as your legacy?

Activity: Take Charge of Your Dreams

Take out your journal and find a quiet place where you will not be disturbed. Set aside at least a half hour for this exercise, or you could do it a little at a time over a period of several days. You may want to create this as a running list and add to it from time to time. Georgia and I keep a list we call our "looking forward to" list. This is where we record all the things that we're looking forward to doing. Since we started doing this we have done more, visited more places, seen more movies and plays, been to more restaurants, and have had more fun than ever.

If you'd like a real challenge, try the exercise from the Jack Canfield and Mark Victor Hansen book, *The Aladdin Factor* (Berkley, 1995). Write out 101 wishes on your dreams list. This will challenge you to really think about everything you want to have, do, become, and share. It is an exercise that is well worth the effort and one that will reward you with a more exciting and fulfilling life.

The secret in completing this activity is to really let your mind go. For the time being, don't be concerned with how you will accomplish these things. All you want to do is brainstorm what it is you would like to be, do, have, and share in your life. Later on we will extract specific goals from the list and create a plan to help you achieve them. For now, all you want to do is let your mind run wild. Become like a child again. If you want to travel to some far-off place, write it down. If you want some new possessions, write them down. If you want a new career, write it down. If you want a fabulous relationship, write it down. If you want to make a difference in your community or in the world, write it down. Whatever you want, write it on your list. It doesn't have to be realistic. Just write down everything that comes to mind. Really stretch yourself beyond your comfort zone!

Your Unique Talents

Each of us has unique gifts or talents that we can share with humanity. Unfortunately, many people devote a lot of time to thinking about the things that they are not good at instead of focusing on those that they do well.

A person will sit thinking that if they could be like someone else or had a specific talent, then they would be happier. Rather than waste your time wishing you were someone else, build upon the gifts and talents that you already possess.

What Are Your Strengths?

Are you great with children? Do you find writing or public speaking something that comes easily to you? Generally our greatest talents are those things that we truly love to do, are naturally good at, and take for granted. There are thousands of different jobs in our society!

When I was a teenager I played bass guitar in a band. I was a fair guitar player but a very good bass player. My friend Bobby was a musician. Being around him I learned the difference between the two, which is why I did not pursue a career in music. Sure, I played professionally for several years and had a lot of fun, but I knew this was not where I would make my mark. I needed to work very hard to learn new songs, because playing music was not something that came easily to me. Bobby, on the other hand, would hear a song once or twice and begin playing it. One day while we were practicing, his younger brother came home from school with a saxophone. Bobby, who at the time played guitar and piano, began fooling around with the sax. Later that evening he was playing songs with it on the stage in the nightclub where we worked. That's a musician!

What are your unique gifts? In your journal begin writing some of the things you enjoy and have a natural ability for. You may well find within this list your ideal work or something that you would enjoy doing as a business. For example, if you enjoy meeting and talking with new people and like to help them, working in a sales capacity or becoming a personal coach might be perfect for you.

Your Lifestyle Business

Many people in our society are taking their passion for something and their natural talents and turning them into successful businesses or careers.

For example, my wife Georgia left her career in telecommunications and returned to her love of fashion and style. She now uses her knowledge of makeup and skin care to help people learn how to look and feel better about themselves. This is a life-long interest she began learning decades ago while working in the London Theatre. She has worked alongside some of the top makeup artists in the business while working as a freelance artist with two leading makeup companies. She published a book of her tips and tricks in 2016 titled *Makeup* (Austin Bay, 2016).

Her years of experience as a corporate trainer and background in theater have made her seminars a huge hit with women's groups and business associations. She loves what she's doing and she is able to combine her experience, talent, and passion into a single pursuit.

Finding Your Passion

If you are entering the workforce for the first time or have children who are doing so, this exercise can be a valuable first step toward finding work that you or they will enjoy. I often speak with young people who are graduating from school and are ready for their first job. Unfortunately, they have been conditioned to use their resumes and try to find some job category they can fit into. I say "unfortunately" because I am of the opinion that there is a better way.

Recently I was speaking with a young woman who was working in a restaurant I frequent. I asked her about her plans now that she finished college. As she began telling me how she was organizing her resume to send out to companies, I could see her expression change to one of pain at the thought of what she had to do. Where there should have been joy, enthusiasm, and excitement at the thought of making her first entrance into the business world, there was only pain and apprehension because she was conditioned to believe she had to make herself fit into an available job. I was quite saddened seeing this bright, energetic woman starting out this way and found myself coaching her about some better ways she could find work she would enjoy.

My belief is that she can find work she will enjoy, be passionate about, and add significant value to whomever hires her.

Several years ago, when my business was slow, I sent my resume to a friend who is an executive recruiter. He called me right away apologetically telling me that he could not help me: "I'm sorry Jim," he said, "I don't have pigeon hole you fit into." After a brief moment of shock, I began to feel really good that I did not fit into any box. I am a gifted human being and have unique talents I can give to the world. The fact that I did not fit the profile is proof to me that I'm on the right track.

6 N

Take Charge of Your Vision

"Vision without action is a daydream. Action without vision is a nightmare."

—JAPANESE PROVERB

*H*elen Keller was asked what it was like not to be able to see; she said, "It's better to have no sight than it is to have no vision."

This is perhaps the most important chapter in this book and surely one of my favorite subjects. It saddens me when I realize just how many people have not taken the time to think about what they want their lives to be five or ten years from now. Many people have not considered where they would like to be and what they would like to be doing even as little as one year from now. Not having a vision of where you are going in your life is like going on vacation by walking out your door, suitcase in hand, getting in your car and driving no place in particular. Most of us would not even consider such a foolish thing, yet we spend more time and energy planning our one and two-week vacations than we do our lives.

Creating a vision for your future is a fun and empowering exercise that will encourage you to expand your sense of what is possible and show you pictures of a bright, abundant future. Pictures which you will then begin to create for yourself.

The Process

In this chapter, I will ask you to invest some time in first creating your "future vision." We will then use your vision to extract some specific goals and milestones and, from those, create shorter term goals and specific action steps which will move you toward your ideal life.

I can hear some of you saying, "But Jim, I do not know what I want to be doing in five years. How can I create a vision?" I understand. I'm not going to ask you to create a structured vision, one where you fill in every little detail. That would take the fun and adventure out of life. I will, however, ask you to create a picture of what your life would look like if you were living your ideal life.

I've chosen five years as the timeframe because it is enough time to make solid plans to create your new reality. You can, of course, do this exercise for longer or shorter periods. When I coach and consult with businesses, we often work with a one-year vision to begin with. The further out in time you can project your vision, the easier it becomes to know what needs to be done now to manifest it. Working back from a five-year vision allows enough time for you to make whatever changes you want to make and to begin from where you are right now. If you want an even greater challenge, do this exercise for twenty years into the future.

From Poverty to Superstar

The world famous actor, Arnold Schwarzenegger, wanted to live in America. He took up weightlifting because it was, at that time, an American sport. Having read about a weightlifter who won the Mr. Universe title and went to America to star as Hercules in a movie, Schwarzenegger decided this would be his way to accomplish his dreams as well. He began by, in his words, "Painting a picture in my mind" of himself standing on a pedestal at the Mr. Universe contest and everyone applauding.

That became his vision. He affirmed that he would win the Mr. Universe title and get into the movies in America. At the time, he was fourteen years old. With his vision held strongly in his mind, he began training to become a world class weight-lifter. When he was twenty years of age, he became the youngest person in history to be crowned Mr. Universe. Three years later he was cast in his first movie, *Hercules in New York*. The rest, as they say, is history.

Andre's Story

Recently, I met a man at the graduation ceremony for a non-profit agency that helps people change their lives. It is an agency I volunteer with and I was honored that I was asked to be the graduation keynote speaker. After my talk, I stood at the back of the room as I listened to each of the graduates from the program tell their stories. Every one of them was a powerful testimonial to the effectiveness of having a clear vision, setting goals, and taking action as a way to change one's life for the better. While each of their stories was powerful, one story sums up the power of having a vision. Standing at the back of the room, tears came to my eyes as I heard one particular man tell his story.

Two years prior to that night, he was homeless and addicted to drugs. It was then that he made a life-altering decision. He decided to seek the help that was available and enrolled in the self-sufficiency program offered by the agency, the Bucks County Opportunity Council. I could feel his pain as he told about his struggle to first get off drugs, and then to get a job and a place to live. He told about the obstacles and challenges he had to overcome to make it through the program—not an easy task for anyone. I had tears in my eyes when he told the audience that night about his new job, wife, and baby girl. In just two short years, this man went from living at the bottom of society to beginning the life of his dreams. He did it by having a vision and by taking the steps necessary to have the life he wanted. The following year, I was again asked to deliver the keynote address. That night I beamed as the man from the previous year told how he was now about to purchase a home for himself and his family.

If you have read my other books you know that my own story is not unlike his. I too was at absolute bottom. By using the ideas and principals I write about, with the help of God, I was able to create what I can only describe today as a dream life. I have been using these principals for years and continue to use them as my life continues to expand and grow. As my reality changes to more closely match my vision, I expand my vision further. There is no top to what one person can accomplish. Is having a vision powerful? You bet it is!

Why We Do This?

In addition to providing you with a road map to your dreams, your vision serves as a way for you to manage your emotional energy. It is pretty well accepted that we attract that which we think about consistently. This, by the way, works whether it is something we want or not. Whatever you focus your attention on day in and day out will eventually come to pass. This is a law, like gravity. By having a clear vision of your future and having identified what you want in your life, you will have created a tool to put yourself in that energy or vibration of attracting that which you want. You will use your vision statement as a powerful affirmation and read it whenever you want to put yourself into the energy of attraction. I personally read my vision each morning before I begin my day. Doing this sets the tone for my day and enables me to start my day in an uplifting state of mind.

The Balancing Act

One of the keys to an exciting, fulfilling, and incredible life is balance. It is important to have balance in your life. Make certain that you include several different areas of your life in your vision. After all, you would not want to be financially successful and lose your family or health would you? Similarly, you would not want to be strong and healthy but living in poverty.

It is important to consider several key areas of your life in order to create a life that is well rounded. As you progress, you will find that you have a tendency to concentrate in one or two specific areas at a time.

The big challenge for most of us is keeping all the parts of our lives in balance. If you focus your attention on your eating and exercise habits, you will become healthier. Unfortunately, when most people do this, they do so at the expense of another part of their life, like finances or family time.

In order to have a truly joyous and successful life, it is important to be growing in each of the key areas. I will ask you to create a vision that includes the main components of a well-balanced life. These are your spirituality or religion; your self-development; your health and fitness; your family, friends, and social relationships; your career and business; social and material goals; and, of course, money and investments. Of course, feel free to modify this list to suit your lifestyle. Notice that I placed money at the end of the list. This is where it belongs, because money is a tool to use. Many people think that they want money, but what they really want is what the money will do for them. Money, by the way, is probably the most explosive issue people face. We will discuss money in more detail in the chapter on your financial destiny, but for now understand that regardless of how you feel about money, it is neither good nor bad.

Creating Your Compelling Vision

You will find the following exercise to be an inspiring and liberating experience that will leave you excited about your life and eager to get moving toward your dreams. That is its purpose, along with providing you with a tool that you can use to align your energy with what you want in your life, thereby greatly increasing the likelihood of you having it. Once you become energetically matched to what it is you want, you begin to draw it to you according to what is known as the law of attraction. The law of attraction, sometimes called the "law of similars" states that "like attracts like." This applies to everything in our lives and is always working whether or not we choose to acknowledge it. This idea has been stated over and over again throughout history. From Proverbs in the Bible, "As a man thinketh in his heart, so is he," to Emerson who said, "A man's what he thinks about all day," to Marcus Aurelius who said, "Our life is what our thoughts make of it."

As I said before, the more you work with your vision and hold your attention on thoughts of that which you want in your life, the faster you will achieve it.

Activity: Your Technicolor Vision

You'll want this to be a fun, exciting exercise—one that will let you really expand your sense of what your life can become. Allow plenty of time to play with these ideas. You may want to complete this exercise over a period of days. Invest some time thinking about what you want your life to be like in five years. Go back to the "dreams" exercise you completed earlier and see what you want to add from there. Make your vision exciting. My friend and coach Terri Levine coined the phrase *Technicolor vision* as a way of encouraging people to create a vibrant tapestry for their life, complete with colors, sounds, and smells. The idea is to really get your juices going, to really excite you each time you read it. For example, there is a tremendous difference in the energy produced by reading the two statements below.

The first one is your typical goal statement, and while it is better than nothing, it does not create the emotion of the second. You can see this for yourself by reading the statements aloud.

"I am so happy driving my new red convertible!"

Or:

"I am thrilled with my new red convertible. I love the feeling of the wind against my face and the smell of the fresh air as I zoom down the highway, with the sound of the wind whooshing by. This feels great!"

Can you feel the difference? Of course you can. The key to creating a powerful vision is to engage as many of your senses as possible. This will produce intense feelings whenever you read it, and these feelings will shift your energy to be in alignment with what you want. Of course, if writing is not something that feels good to you, then you can draw your vision on a piece of paper or speak it into a tape recorder. Use whatever media will inspire you to paint a rich tapestry for your life. You could use a treasure map and make a visual collage, using pictures of what you want in your life. For more about treasure maps see Chapter 9: "Take Charge of Your Personal Power."

When creating your vision, make it rich, colorful, vibrant, exciting, and engaging. Be sure to use your sense of sight, hearing, touch, and smell. Make it a Technicolor vision. As I said earlier, we will, for the sake of this exercise, use a five-year time-frame. You can, of course, create a vision for shorter or longer time periods as well. In working with businesses we create a vision for the business and then each person on the team creates their vision that is in align-ment with the company's vision.

Below are some examples taken from my own life's vision and those of some of the great coaches I've had the good fortune to have known and work with.

Sandie's Vision

I love my life; it is awesome and wonderful, flowing with ease, grace, joy, freedom, creativ-ity, inspiration, trust, acceptance, and gratitude. I am grateful and happy. I recognize, trust, and honor my inner source of abundance and, together with the positive abundance of the universe, I allow myself to co-create infinite wealth and perpetual prosperity.

My business thrives—clients come and find me, income grows and exceeds expectations. I am thrilled and enchanted with my delightful success. I'm an inspired and creative soul who leads with my heart as well as my head and my hands. I envision and sculpt my own life with awesome brilliance, tapping my intuition, wisdom, and passion in ways that allow me to share my gifts with the world. I live with powerful and purposeful intention, owning my spirituality with simplicity and elegance in ways that flow to a positive difference, serving me and everyone I interact with for the highest good.

To learn more about Sandie Pinches visit www .aboveandbeyondcoaching.com.

Siobhan's Vision

This has been a marvelous year. It's my best year ever. I've never been clearer about my mission, values, needs, and gifts. My body looks fantastic and feels even better. My sense of vitality and well-being has expanded and grown. I have all the energy I need and I love hiking, biking, swimming, skiing, and being outdoors. I love feeling beautiful and free in the great clothes I wear. They fit great and wear well.

My husband and I are connected at an even deeper level. We've had some great trips together and attended a fabulous couple's workshop and are deeply committed to each other.

We love our home and feel so peaceful in it. It is clutter free and beautifully and comfortably decorated. All the inhabitants and visitors feel a sense of harmony and peace when they are in our home. We enjoy entertaining and sharing this space with our loved ones. Lots of laughing and dancing are the norm!

I'm confident in all the methods I've chosen to express my vision and mission. My business is focused on my unique abilities and brilliance! I coach extraordinary people who are in sync with what I have to offer. My practice has only ideal clients who are ready and able to implement the tools I share with them. They love to send me checks and gifts! I feel so appreciated and they receive so much value! I work on a select number of exciting projects per year that are deeply satisfying and fulfilling.

I am handsomely paid for work I love doing. This year I feel ecstatic as I double my revenue! I feel so abundant as I tithe ten percent of my income. I know I can't out-give God!

Through it all, I have plenty of time and space for rejuvenation, spirit time, and play. I keep a weekly artist date with myself. Our social life is fulfilling and manageable including time with family, friends, and key relationships.

To learn more about Siobhan Murphy, visit www.questcoaching.com.

Jim's Vision

My life is awesome! My health is fantastic. I beam with energy and look and feel fit, trim, and healthy. I look fantastic. I honor and love my body and take great care of it. I always have boundless energy. I jump out of bed early each day, eager to greet the new day. I feel so vibrant and healthy.

I am jazzed about my work. My books and programs fly off the shelves reaching and helping millions of people throughout the world. This feels great.

I have tears of joy each time I hear a story of someone who has changed their life for the better because of something I wrote or said. I create new books with ease and joy and they reach people across the globe.

My work is having a massive positive effect on the lives of people everywhere, and I am honored and thrilled that I earn huge sums of money for writing books and delivering seminars that help people grow. I feel fantastic doing this. I feel so successful and appreciated. My life is magnificent, and I love every minute of it.

Balancing Your Vision

In your vision, be sure to include something from each of the following categories:

Spiritually and Religion

In five years, where are you spiritually? What is your relationship to your Creator? Do you spend time each day in prayer and meditation? Are you involved with your church, synagogue, or mosque? Are you living a spiritual life? How is this being reflected in your day-to-day life? What is your connection to your community? Where do you give back?

Self-development

What have you done to enrich your mind? Have you added to your education? Did you obtain a degree or learn a new skill? Have you studied a new language? What are you doing regularly to expand your mind? How many books have you read? How many audios have you listened to? Have you attended a seminar or webinar on a particular subject? Do you make a habit of reading uplifting, inspirational material each day? Doing this for just fifteen minutes a day will help you keep a positive attitude and will contribute more to your success than any other action you can take.

Health and Fitness

How is your health? Are you becoming more fit? What are you doing to nurture yourself regularly? Do you exercise? What about sports and leisure activities? Have you taken up a sport, such as golf or tennis? Are you steadily improving your eating habits to become healthier? Do you have regular medical checkups? Are you taking extraordinary care of your body? Do you have massages, facials, or other types of body work? Do you take time for yourself and actively work to reduce stress? Have you studied yoga, tai chi, qi gong, or something to help you relax and increase your physical fitness?

Family and Relationships

What about your relationships? Do you have a great relationship with your spouse and loved ones? What about friends? Have you developed meaningful relationships with people who support you and have your best interests in mind? Are you supportive and nurturing to your friends as well? Have you found ways to maintain romance in your significant relationship?

Career and Business

In your five-year vision, where have you gone in your career or business? What is your work day like? What are the feelings you experience in your chosen work? How great is it? Have you begun your own business? How has it grown? What are you doing each day? Where are you contributing to society? Remember the idea of a big vision, one that will excite you just thinking about living it.

Social and Material

What are you doing socially? Have you seen a number or plays, concerts, or movies? Where are you vacationing? Have you taken your family to a great restaurant? What are you doing? What do you own? Do you have a new luxury automobile? A boat? A plane? A summer house at the beach? Have you added an incredible media center to your home? A new computer? New furniture? A great wardrobe? Do you have a special piece of jewelry or watch that you've always wanted? What have you been able to buy for your family?

Money and Investments

How much money are you earning? What have you invested in? How much are you saving each month? What are you using your money for? Have you set aside the money for your children's education? Are you tithing regularly?

These are just some examples of the kinds of questions that you may want to ask yourself as you create your personal vision. Make it big, bright, powerful, and exciting. As the late Norman Vincent Peale, considered to be one the pioneers of the modern self-help movement, said, "If you want a big life, you need big dreams."

Great! You now have an inspiring, motivating, rich vision of how you want your life to be in five years. I strongly suggest that you take the time to read it each day. This act alone will begin to draw it toward you and greatly increase your chance of it becoming a reality. Reading your vision with excitement and passion will also help you begin each day with your personal energy in alignment with what you most want, thereby attracting it toward you. You may even want to record this and play it back for yourself. Remember the universe works on the principal of like attracts like. The more you put yourself in the energetic state of that which you want and experience the feelings of having it, the more you will attract it to you.

Breaking It Down

Now that you have a clear idea of where you want to be and what you want your life to become, it is time to extract some specific measurable goals you can achieve in the next twelve months. We will then break these down even further and, finally, develop an action plan to keep you on track.

Looking back over each area of your vision find one or two specific goals that are in alignment with your overall vision. Goals that you can accomplish in a year's time that will move you toward fulfilling your vision. For example, if in your vision you are living a carefree life, with plenty of money, doing work you love, a one-year goal that would lead you toward your vision might be to start your own business and begin earning a specific amount of money from it.

Write your goal in the present tense as though it has already happened and state it in the positive. Be sure to make it exciting and colorful too. Your one-year career goal might look like this, "I am so excited having my successful business, making a difference, and earning an additional twenty-five thousand dollars a year from it."

If in your vision you have a great, loving, supportive, respectful, special relationship with another person, your goal might look like this: "I am so happy that I am in a warm, loving, passionate relationship with the perfect person for me." Another might be, "I am blessed with supportive and loving friends whom I enjoy spending time with."

In your journal complete this exercise, choosing one or two goals from each of the areas in your vision. Think about what goal or milestone you could accomplish in one year that will support your five-year vision. By the way, if you already have your own business, you may want to complete a vision and goal session for it, and if you have employees or a team, have each of them do the same. Companies using these principals have produced quantum leaps in their revenue. As I said before, you can use these techniques for any area of your life.

The alternative is leaving your life to chance. The fact that you're reading this book tells me that you are not one of those people willing to settle and live, as Henry David Thoreau said, "in quiet desperation." You have within you the power to change your life, and within this book are the tools and techniques to help you do it.

Breaking It Further Down

Once again I'm going to ask you to extract measurable specific goals. This time you will look at your one-year goals and ask what you can accomplish in three months. Take each goal that you set earlier and break it down into a three-month milestone. For example, in your business area, your one-year goal of highly successful business could become a three-month goal like the following: "I have happily begun my new business part-time and it is growing steadily." Your relationship goal may become something like this: "I am so happy having met a wonderful person whom I enjoy being with." Again, do this for each of the one-year goals you identified. I realize this seems like a lot of work, but it will be well worth it. This is one of the best activities you can do for yourself. You are really taking charge of your destiny and creating the life you want to live. You may want to do this with your family and those people close to you, especially your children. You're almost finished with the vision and goals portion of this book, so at this time you may want to give yourself a break. I want to congratulate you for doing these exercises for yourself.

One-month Goals and Action Steps

One of the "secrets" to creating a life that you've always wanted, accomplishing your goals, and making your dreams come true is taking regular focused action toward their achievement.

You have created a long-term vision, set your one-year goals based on that vision, and then broken those goals into smaller three-month goals. We will now take it one step further. Look at your three-month goals and see what you can do in the next thirty days to move toward this accomplishment. Then, write each of these on an index card, using a separate card for each goal area. These are something you can carry with you and read whenever you want.

You may want to complete a mini version of this exercise for a specific area of your life. I have a mini version for my books and writing, as well as my seminars and coaching programs. I also have one for my health and fitness goals. These simple tools help keep me focused and on track as I actively create the life I want to live. As the title of this book suggests, it is time to take charge of your destiny.

I use my cards like this: On one side of the card I write the goal in an exciting and positive way, being sure to put a great deal of emotion into it, include why I want this, and how I will feel when it is accomplished.

Then, on the other side I list specific actions that I will take during the next thirty days that will move me toward making the goal a reality. After using these cards for a period of time, I discovered some interesting things. Before I begin my day or prior to working on a particular area I will read the card. This puts me in the high, positive emotional state, and I'm already attracting what I want to me. Additionally, I found when I do this and then turn the card over and read my actions, more often than not I will think of another small action that I can take to move me toward my desired outcome. I call this inspired action.

For example, in working with the card for my seminar, as I read my goal and looked at my list of actions, I was inspired to contact a non-profit agency and discuss how I might help them by leveraging my seminars. This "inspired action" will produce additional income for me and help the struggling charity raise some much needed money.

The reason this is so effective is that by first reading your passionate goal you create a mental and emotional state that is conducive to creativity. The ideas that come while you are in that state tend to be more inspired and creative then what you might normally think to do. The more passionate and excited you are about your goals and the more you're in that state of feeling as though they have already happened, the more you are tapping into the higher guidance that is available to us all. Your subconscious mind will go to work to find new ways for you to accomplish your goals. Doors will open. The right people will come into your life. All sorts of things will occur to help you along your path.

If you find this idea a bit too far out, I challenge you to use it for a few months and see if you don't agree that the actions you are being inspired to take are significantly more creative than you have been used to. As with everything I've written here, this is not just a nice theory.

All of the ideas, tools, and techniques presented here have been used successfully by myself and others. I have never written anything without first using it in my own life for validation. I believe that this is one of the reasons people have responded so well to my books. I am able to write with certainty, having appointed myself as the guinea pig in my own life's experiment.

This completes this section on creating your vision and establishing a simple system and plan for making it a reality. If you have not completed these activities please go back and do so now. This is, perhaps, one of the most important steps that you will take toward taking charge of your destiny and creating the life you were born to live.

7

Take Charge of Your Health

*"Disease cannot live in
a healthy body."*
—NORMAN WALKER

No book dealing with personal growth would be complete without at least touching on the subject of health, because without our health it is impossible to achieve the other things we want.

Too many people never have the kind of life they want and deserve simply because they run out of energy before they get where they are going.

Many people in our world today are in less than optimal health; however, much of this can be corrected with some simple lifestyle changes. Even people in countries that were once renowned for their health such as Japan, Korea, China, Italy, and France are now developing many of the debilitating diseases of the West due to the introduction of American fast food, with its high fat content and unhealthy ingredients, into these countries.

Most people's lifestyles in the twenty-first century do not include enough physical exercise and movement.

Much of the physical labor of the past provided us with a baseline of physical exercise which has since been replaced by technology and modern conveniences in much of the developed world. Our youth are playing video games representing the sports their parents and grandparents used to play live. In America, a frightening percentage of our children are considered to be obese, and the problem does not seem to be getting any better as our diets are increasingly comprised of fat and sugar.

All one needs to do is examine the typical shopping cart in a supermarket to see this problem clearly. America, I am saddened to say, is a nation of junk food eaters.

My Turning Point

If you really want to take charge of your destiny and create the life you were born to live, developing a health plan is an important component. While I make no claims as a medical or health professional, I have studied health and nutrition, as an avocation, for over 35 years. I was first introduced to the idea of health and nutrition by my friend Charlie Blackmore. I remember one day many years ago, when I had been living in California, saying to Charlie, "I feel awful. What can I do about it?" He said that if I placed my trust in him and followed his suggestions I would feel better. We were roommates at the time, and I became a willing participant in his health experiment. He and I were to be the test subjects in his health experiment. We both began taking large doses of vitamins each day. I was introduced to things such as juicing, bee pollen, ginseng, and numerous other (strange to this guy from New York City) substances. Charlie would also spend endless hours browsing natural food stores. Thus began my interest in health and nutrition. I have to honestly say that I believe that one of the reasons I survived my past lifestyle of excess was because, aside from drinking and smoking heavily, I took good care of my health. Today, all things considered, I am quite healthy and steadily improving each day. Of course,

I no longer drink or smoke and play an active part in assuring my future wellbeing.

A New Model for a Healthy Life

In the past, in most cultures people went to their family doctor when they were ill and, hopefully, did whatever he (most doctors were men) said. While this is still true for many people, there are two problems. One, people tend to expect the doctor to make them well without taking responsibility for their own health, and second, many people do not even follow their doctor's advice, expecting instead to be given a "magic pill."

This is pure nonsense. We are each responsible for our own health and well-being. It is unfair to our doctors to give them this responsibility. Like every other area of your life, if you want to have the power to change it, you must first be willing to take responsibility for it. When I began writing this book I was heavier than I am now. This was largely a result of slipping slowly back into some old eating habits and not exercising. I was responsible for having gained the extra weight; therefore, I knew I could lose it. By the time this book was finished, I had lost the weight. I simply set a goal and wrote it in my journal. I then developed an action plan that, for me, included writing a food diary each day to keep track of what I was eating. I then increased my physical exercise. It is interesting to note that the one common trait among people who have lost a significant amount of weight and kept it off is that they all maintained a food journal.

Healthy Role Models

As I have suggested before, finding role models who serve as guides to help you reach your goals is a great way to keep yourself motivated. For me, my good friend and attorney, Jim Sutton, is one of them. Jim is a marathon runner who works out at his gym six days a week and runs on the seventh. When I don't feel like going to the health club, all I have to do is think about him and it motivates me to get going. We all need role models. I figure if he has time to work out six or seven days a week, I can surely manage four or five.

One day at my health club, I spoke with one of the staff, a young woman named Leah Dillon. When she mentioned that she worked out almost every day I asked her how she got herself to do that, as working out every day seemed pretty extreme to me. Her answer inspired me to begin seeing myself at a new level of fitness. She said, "I want to know what it would feel like to be in the best physical condition of my life, just one time." Wow! What a concept. Inspired by her statement, I recently reset my exercise goals.

Achieving Your Personal Best

Imagine achieving your own personal best with regard to health and fitness. How great would that be? I'm not talking about trying to fit into the media's idea of how you should look. I'm suggesting that you create your ideal body and your best health so that you can live your life filled with health and energy.

Your Health Team

In my opinion, life is not so much about how long we live as it is the quality of life we have for however long we are on this earth. To achieve this I have created a concept I call "My Health Team." Rather than put the responsibility for my life in the hands of my doctor, I have chosen to take personal responsibility for it and have assembled a team of health practitioners and advisors. You see, while I believe the medical profession, at least in the United States, is very good at diagnosing and treating illness and excellent at emergency medicine, I feel there is a big difference between not being sick and being healthy.

Many people in our world today might be considered "not sick," because they have no overt symptoms and are feeling alright. However, that is not to say that they are healthy. While doctors for the most part are great at helping you if have an illness, it is not within the scope of their work to treat a well person. For this reason I have assembled my own team of health professionals.

Because I believe the one who is ultimately accountable for my health is me, I have appointed myself captain of my own health team. Depending upon your present level of health and fitness and your beliefs about the subject, your team members will vary from person to person. My own personal team includes, of course, our family doctor and, when necessary, one or more specialists and my dentist.

I have also included a nutritionist who uses an advanced type of computerized diagnostic system to identify imbalances and correct them before they become problems. At various times, my team will include a massage therapist, my local natural food store, personal coach, health club, chiropractor, personal trainer, yoga teacher, and various other energy modalities to help me stay balanced.

By employing the concept of a "health team" I am able to maintain the best health possible and continue to improve as time goes on.

In addition to my health team, I eat a reasonably healthy diet and supplement that with a number of vitamins, herbs, and some of the cutting edge nutrients like Coenzyme Q10, a powerful antioxidant. Stephen Sinatra, M.D., a leading cardiologist and the author of several books including *The Coenzyme Q10 Phenomenon* (Keats Publishing 1998), said that in his research, Co-enzyme Q10 was one of the greatest medical advances of the 20th century for the treatment of heart disease.

I exercise regularly and, as I said earlier, I've been inspired to set a goal of being in the best physical condition I have ever been. The interesting thing about this goal is that I can never reach it. It will keep moving as I approach it. The more fit I become, the more I increase my fitness capacity. This is one goal that I will enjoy never reaching.

One last thought about health and fitness. You may be thinking, "I'm getting older; it's too late for me to get fit." Studies have shown that, regardless of your age when you begin exercising, you can increase your fitness levels dramatically by following a regular exercise regimen. Of course, check with your healthcare professional before starting any exercise or nutritional program.

Activity:
Your Health Team

Think about your own health and fitness. What types of team members would help you become your personal best? Could a yoga or tai chi teacher help you add more flexibility in your body? Would you benefit from the services of a personal trainer? When was the last time you had a physical examination? Men in particular tend to be very lax about this, as do certain ethnic groups, such as my Irish relatives. Are your eating habits something that would benefit from a nutritional counselor? Could an herbologist be just what you need to help with a specific health issue?

In your journal, identify the members of your personal health team, even if you do not presently know who they are. Just think about what kinds of specialties would help you achieve your health goals and live a healthier life filled with an abundant energy.

In addition to establishing your personal health team and embarking on a regular exercise program, there are some other steps you can take to maintain and improve your health:

Eat a Well-balanced Diet

I believe, and health experts will agree, that most foods can be eaten in moderation. Problems arise when people eat foods high in fat or sugar as the main component in their diet. Most Westerns eat much too much red meat, a habit that has managed to invade the otherwise healthy diets of Asian people as well with the introduction of American food chains. While eating a small amount of red meat a couple of times a week is probably fine for the average person, eating large amounts of it contributes to high blood pressure, high cholesterol, and clogged arteries. Instead, add healthy servings of fish, especially salmon, rich in essential fats and oils, to your diet. Of course, eating large amounts of fresh fruits and vegetables is great, as they are packed with nutrients. Buying organic produce is a good idea whenever possible. Soy and whole grains are another good addition to our diets as they are high in protein and fiber and low in fat. The key to a healthy diet is quite simple—use common sense.

Drink Plenty of Water

The one thing every medical and health practitioner will agree on is that most people do not drink enough pure water. When I refer to water, I mean water—not coffee, tea, or soda. While they contain water, they are not perceived by the body as water and do not count. Drinking at least eight to ten glasses of water a day has many health benefits. Most physical therapists and chiropractors will tell you that many of their patients would have less back pain if only they drank more water. Water helps hydrate the disks between our spinal vertebrae, which can become dehydrated and cause pain. It also aids in digestion and helps flush toxins out of our bodies.

Virtually all weight loss programs emphasize the healthy benefits of water and the part it plays in maintaining a healthy weight. Personally I find it quite easy to drink a lot of water. I always have a large bottle with me at the health club and keep a big mug of water on my desk at home. Once you develop a habit of drinking plenty of water, you will find that it is something your body wants and it becomes automatic. Adding a fresh lemon gives the water a pleasant taste and it adds the healthy benefits of the lemon, high in vitamin C and bioflavonoids.

Take Time to Breathe

Most people breathe in a very shallow way. There is a wonderful breathing exercise by Andrew Weil, M.D., author of the *New York Times* bestseller, *Spontaneous Healing*. It is taken from Pranayoga and is called the "relaxing breath."

Dr. Weil says it is the most powerful relaxation method he knows and one he teaches every patient he works with. Quite simply, you inhale through your nose quietly and exhale through your mouth. Begin by exhaling through your mouth completely, in order to empty your lungs of air. Next, inhale quietly through your nose for a count of four. Hold your breath for a count of seven and exhale through your mouth for a count of eight. What is important here is not the length of time, but the ratio four, seven, eight for the inhalation, holding, and exhalation.

Of course if you are under the care of a medical doctor, please check with them before beginning this or any exercise. To reap the long term benefits of relaxing breath do a minimum of four cycles, twice a day. After a month you can increase the number of cycles to eight, but never do more than eight breath cycles. This is a very powerful technique and can have a profound effects on physiology. Of course, if you become out of breath or feel dizzy, stop immediately.

Quiet Time and Relaxation

Our entire society is on overdrive. People are rushing through their lives as though the goal was to get to the end, all the while missing the joy along the way. Happiness is a journey, not a destination. To have a full and rewarding life, we need to learn to enjoy every moment of it, not live for some far off future destination. One way to learn to slow the pace of your life in order to fully enjoy and appreciate it is to devote some time each day to quiet reflection, prayer, and meditation. Spending time in quiet relaxation is one of the best things we can do for ourselves. Not only does it have enormous health benefits, helping to lower your heart rate and blood pressure, but it's one of the keys to tapping into your creative potential.

Sit for Ideas

The great inventor Thomas Edison used to close his office door and "sit for ideas" on a regular basis. He would simply instruct his staff that he was not to be disturbed and sit quietly in a chair for up to two hours at a time. This kind of quiet contemplation allows your creative mind to come up with ideas and solve problems. In this quiet state, you are able to access your intuitive mind.

Whatever changes you make to your diet and lifestyle, the important thing to remember is to start taking responsibility for your health. If you want to have the life of your dreams, your physical and mental health are a significant part of it. Take charge of your health and fitness as you continue to take charge of your destiny and to create the life you were born to live.

Set some specific goals right now to help you achieve your "personal best" level of health and fitness. Remember to check with your doctor or health practitioner before beginning any diet or exercise program, then develop your personal plan for achieving the level of health you want. Starting right now, plan to incorporate time each day for quiet time, prayer time, relaxation, or meditation and make this part of your overall health plan.

8

Take Charge of Your Finances

"You cannot get rich without enriching others."

—Andrew Carnegie

While it is not within the scope of this book to be a financial treatise, I would like to devote some time and space to a brief discussion of finances and how you can help yourself become more financially secure and, ultimately, financially independent. Finances are the greatest source of stress in people's lives and are probably responsible for more marital relationship problems than anything else.

Money is a core issue in our society among everyone regardless of their income level.

I've always liked the principle I learned from Robert T. Kiyosaki and Sharon L. Lechter regarding finance. They call it "getting out of the rat race." If you really want to learn more about this topic, I highly recommend reading the *Rich Dad, Poor Dad* series of books. It will change your perspective about wealth and money. Being out of the "rat race" means that you have sufficient passive income to support your lifestyle and pay all of your expenses. This is income you receive whether or not you actively work. In other words, having residual, asset, or royalty income to support your lifestyle. This gives you the freedom to pursue whatever it is you want to pursue in life. There are several ways to achieve this.

A Painful Lesson

A while back I learned two very valuable lessons about finances. It was during the dot com boom and I had invested money in a high-technology stock, which I purchased for $53 a share. Fortunately for me, I did not purchase a lot of it, so while the lesson was an expensive one it was not devastating. I sat one day as the stock reached $65 a share and a little voice inside of me said, "This would be a good time to sell it, take my profit, and go do something else with the money."

Before I could act on that small voice within, the one we generally consider to be our intuition or instinct (and the one that is usually accurate), another little voice, this time from my head (which I will label my greedy voice), said, "Hold on, it may go even higher." That was on a Tuesday morning, and that particular stock started to go steadily down from $65 a share until it finally bottomed out, or more accurately, I got out at $1.50 a share, losing a considerable amount of money along the way.

I learned two very valuable lessons from this experience. The first lesson was to trust my instincts and not let greed get in my way. My first instinct was the accurate one that would have allowed me to get out with a profit. The second lesson, which is even more important, is to not go into things that I do not fully understand. While I have a cursory knowledge of the stock market, I don't consider myself to be an expert. If and when I ever go into stock investing again, I will have gained the expertise necessary to make it profitable. Like any other industry, the stock market works with specialized information and the people who understand it and know how to play the game make money.

Another financial author's work I admire is Suzy Orman. She wrote *The Courage to be Rich* (Bantam Doubleday) and a series of financial books and is now a big TV star dispensing financial advice. My only challenge with Suzy is that part of her plan is to cut back on your expenses by drinking cheaper coffee and having fewer personal services. I personally don't like that concept. I much prefer the Kiyosaki model, which is "Live within in your means and raise your means." That suits me and my lifestyle much better. I enjoy the finer things that this life has to offer, and why shouldn't I? And why shouldn't you, for that matter?

One of Kiyosaki's metaphors struck me as if someone had dropped a brick on my head because it was so simple and so obvious. If you're not starting with a lot of money and are, like most of people, working for a living, the way to create wealth is to create assets that will produce income. This income can then be used to purchase other assets and liabilities. A liability, in his view, is something that costs you money rather than provides it. Things like cars, boats, airplanes, and jewelry are liabilities. His suggestion is to delay buying expensive luxuries until you can pay for them with asset income. This way, you are not buying liabilities with your labor.

Creating Assets

The very book you're reading is an asset I created. While my purpose for writing books is more about sharing information to help people than about money, I can honestly say that I have been very fortunate and have made a significant amount of money from my books. It has afforded me a very nice lifestyle. At the same time, I have had a positive effect on the lives of hundreds of thousands of people throughout the world. To me, this is the ultimate success.

While I may be able to write books and create assets, what do you do if you're not a writer? There are lots of other options. One of them is network marketing.

Network marketing is one of the few industries that you can go into with actually little or no money and become, if you have the desire and the drive, independently wealthy. I know several people who are multi-millionaires today, having started with nothing more than a burning desire to succeed in network marketing.

Something else that you can do is learn about making money with real estate investments. Many wealthy real estate investors started by buying small pieces of property, which produced a positive cash flow. Over time, they were able to leverage their investment and purchase additional properties. Real estate is interesting because it is the only investment that I have seen where the bank will give you the majority of the purchase price. I can't imagine going into the bank and saying, "I want to buy stock in this bank and I'd like you to loan me 90 percent of the money." They would laugh you out the door. However, if you walk in with a piece of property and say, "I want to buy this piece of property and I would like to borrow 90 percent of the money," most banks, at least in the US, will gladly give it to you. That's a general indicator of the value of real estate because, as people have said, they aren't making any more of it. What there is, is what there is. One of the reasons waterfront property is so expensive in most of the world is because it is in very limited supply.

Becoming Debt-free

No discussion on finance would be complete without at least a mention about debt and the problems it can cause. I know this firsthand because I have had more than my share of it and have spent a period of time eliminating the debt in my life. I suggest to anyone who wants to have a stress-free life—especially if you want to be financially independent—that you make a priority of reducing the debt that you have and not incurring any new debt.

One of the ways to do this is to take the amount of money that you can afford to pay each month on your total debt and divide it by the number of credit cards you have. Then, make the minimum payment on every card other than the card with the highest interest rate. Pay the remainder of your budget on that card until it is paid off. Then move on to the next highest rate card, and so on.

This very simple debt reduction system is taught by Debtors Anonymous and every other program that helps people get out of debt. I will say here, if you are deeply in debt, that you get some help. Find some agency or group that can help you learn to manage your debt. Many people are deeply in debt because of a gambling problem. If this is your case, by all means get professional help; go to Gamblers Anonymous (www.gamblersanonymous .org). Gambling is a serious illness like alcoholism and drug addiction and needs to be treated as such. If you feel that you have a problem, do something about it. Don't let it destroy your life.

Your Financial Future

One sure way to financial freedom is owning your own business, even if it's only part-time. If you look at the statistics of self-made millionaires, you'll discover that the majority of them are small business owners.

In our uncertain employment climate, it is more important than ever to have a measure of control over your income, and being an independent business owner is one of the best ways to accomplish this. The average family would be living better with less stress and more enjoyment if they earned an extra few hundred dollars a month. This can easily be accomplished by owning your own part-time business.

Aside from the financial rewards of your own business, you gain peace of mind and a sense of security knowing that no matter what you have some control over your income. If something were to suddenly happen to your job you would at least have something to fall back on. With so many companies downsizing today, this is more important than ever.

Keeping an Evidence Journal

Often we do not even notice the abundance that we already have in our lives. We tend to forget all the little signs that the universe is, in fact, supporting us. One way to begin to see and appreciate the abundance that is flowing into your life, and a way to attract more, is to start keeping an evidence journal. An evidence journal is simply a running record of any money that comes into your life. If you receive a gift of money, record it in your journal. If you find a small amount of money on the street, write that in your evidence journal too.

Doing this serves several purposes. For one, it draws your attention to the abundance that you are receiving, thereby creating a feeling of gratitude. And it serves as a sign that you are in fact increasing your wealth. This can be likened to a ship at sea. When land approaches, the ship begins to see driftwood floating in the water. The driftwood is a sign that land is close by. If you just started a new business, you will not see the financial rewards for a time; however, by recording any amounts money you receive you will be noticing the "driftwood." Remember, we get more of what we focus upon. If you want more money notice the money that you are already receiving. Something else that I like about keeping an evidence journal is that I can look back at it and see just how fortunate I am and how much the universe has supported me. This always makes me feel better.

Change Box

One of the ideas that I've implemented from Susie Orman's *Courage to be Rich* book is to begin collecting change. Whenever I purchase something, I always use paper money, even though I may have coins in my pocket. At the end of the day I deposit these coins into a change box that I keep in my dresser. When the box is filled I take it to the bank and cash it in. I then take the money, usually around $200, and buy something nice for myself or my wife or donate it to a worthwhile charity.

Sometimes we use the money to go out to a nice restaurant. By saving the coins each day, I do not even notice the amount of money as it builds into a small nest egg. I know of people who do this for an entire year and use the collected coins to pay for a family vacation.

Spending Record

Have you ever looked into your wallet or hand-bag at the end of the day and wondered where the money went? I know I have. We tend to go through our day purchasing items like newspapers, coffee, tea, magazines, candy, soft drinks, snacks, etc. without giving much thought to it. If you really want to gain a sense of where your money goes, you may want to use a spending record. What this means is that for one month you record every purchase you make regardless of its size. Get a small pad or use an app and keep a running record of each and every purchase you make throughout the day. Keeping a spending record for a month or two is a great way to gain control over your spending.

Discuss Finances Openly

In completing this chapter about finances, I would like to offer a suggestion. Talk openly about money and finances with your family. Had more of us learned about money and finances growing up, we would have been better equipped for the world that lay ahead.

I don't know about you, but the only references I ever heard about money growing up were that other people had more than we did and that there was never enough. These and other negative messages given to young people set them up for financial struggle or, at best, a poor understanding about how money works.

It is interesting to note that very wealthy people, the rich and ultra-rich, begin educating their children about money at a young age. These young people become astute financial stewards by the time they're adults and are able to manage and secure their financial future.

Although most of the messages that I received about money growing up were negative, I did learn some positive ones. I learned that if I was willing to work for it, I could earn pretty much what I wanted. Money to me as a young person meant independence and freedom, so I found ways to earn whatever money I needed. As a teenager I was doing quite well financially. A side benefit to this was that I discovered that I could easily learn new tasks. Both of these beliefs, created in my early teens, have served me well over the years.

Taking the time now to teach your children about finances will go a long way toward ensuring their successful financial future.

9

Take Charge of Your Personal Power

"Great spirits have always
encountered violent opposition
from mediocre minds."
—ALBERT EINSTEIN

*W*hen was the last time you took a "self-care day" just for yourself? Doing this means taking one 24-hour period where you take exceptional care of yourself. You do no work at all. I know, I can hear your protest. I protested too when I first heard this idea "But you don't understand, I have to check my email, I have to return phone calls, I have to post on Facebook, and on and on." I protested in my very best entrepreneurial voice. The truth is any of us can take a day for ourselves without consequence. Believe it or not, the world will keep spinning. Calls will wait and so will email.

This is a day just for you. If you normally do the cooking, on your extraordinary self-care day you will refrain from making meals. Trust me, your family will not starve. Obviously if there are small children or infants who depend on you, you would have to modify this. Perhaps you can have someone else feed them for this one day. Overall try to do nothing that is related to your normal work. This is a pampering day just for you.

The first time I did this, I discovered just how my work relates to things that I do on any given day. Most of my reading was centered on business topics. Being an entrepreneur and self-employed, I was convinced I had to be working all the time. I was wrong. Kicking and screaming, I embarked on my self-care day. I took a walk, read part of a novel, took a luxurious bath in our soaking tub (something I never used to do), and just relaxed and took care of myself. What a concept!

It's been a few years now and my self-care day has become an integral part of my life. I not only feel better and am having more fun, I have my life back.

Doing this regularly has enabled me to put my work back into perspective. I no longer work seven days a week, and I no longer do email throughout the day.

The interesting thing is that because of my taking this time to nurture myself, I'm actually more productive. Because I'm taking better care of myself, I have more clarity and I'm able to better focus on the task at hand.

Because I am taking better care of myself, I am more creative and productive. Most of all, because I am taking better care of myself I feel better and have more happiness. After all, isn't that what it's all about?

Activity:
Your Self-care Day

Schedule one 24-hour period, sometime within the next 10 days, when you can give yourself an extraordinary self-care day. Once you've done this, see how you might be able to do this weekly.

Powerful Questions

Each week my wife and I sit down and complete a simple exercise I learned from the book

Breaking the Rules (CPM Publishing, 1998) by Kurt Wright. In this book, he uses a five-question process that I feel is truly brilliant in its ability to focus a person's attention in the direction that they want to go. Georgia and I use the question, "What's working?" as a way to shift our focus away from anything that may not be quite right in our respective businesses or relationship and toward those things that are working. We write a list of everything we can think of that is going right. Sometimes it's a short list, but more often it's quite long and filled with exciting opportunities.

Doing this accomplishes two very important things. First it leaves us feeling good about what we are doing. Often people are focused on the things that are not working and they wonder why they are depressed.

As we each discuss and write out what is going right, we automatically begin to feel better. This in turn attracts more of that to us. Remember that you get more of what you focus upon. This is the law of attraction. Like attracts like. So if you are consistently focusing on what is going right, you will see more of that and begin to attract more of the same.

Applying the Principle

I want to delve a little further into how you can use this for any area of your life, as well as your business. As I have said before, I work on steadily improving my health; however, there are times when I feel that I am not making as much progress as I would like or times when I have slacked off on my fitness program. When this happens I'll do a "What's working?" exercise for my health.

I will begin listing all the things that I am doing that are moving me toward my goal of ideal health. My particular list may include things such as going to the health club four or five days a week, following a balanced food program, eliminating caffeine, reducing sugar, taking a yoga class, seeing my nutritionist, having a massage, and so on. No matter how long or short my list is at any particular time, it causes me to focus my attention on those things that are working, which causes me to feel better and moves me further along toward my goal.

This one simple question can be used in any situation for any part of your life. You can use it with your spouse, children, or co-workers. If you use this in a business situation, be prepared to see some strange expressions on the faces of your co-workers. We have become so conditioned to asking the exact opposite that the question alone causes people to stop and think.

How many times have you been at a meeting at work when your boss or someone will say something like "Okay, sales are down, what's wrong?" Everyone immediately starts searching their brains for reasons why they are not getting the results they want. They come up with all sorts of reasons why things are wrong. They then leave the meeting feeling down and depressed, having just spent a lot of time and energy looking at things that do not work. If this happens to be a sales meeting, you are then expected to go out and sell.

You could not possibly be in a worse frame of mind to sell successfully than after having attended a meeting like that. Has this ever happened to you? I'm guessing it has. While there is some value in knowing what does not work, there is absolutely no value in constantly going over it. To continue to feel good and move steadily in a direction of your dreams and desires, remain focused on what is working and build upon that.

More Questions to Ask

While asking "what's working" will keep you focused on what you want to attract, there is added value in using the complete question framework as described in Wright's book, which I highly recommend reading if you want to learn more about this subject.

1. *Why is it working?*

In working on your business you may have listed such things as networking and word of mouth, brochures, direct mail, and a website as "what's working" to build your business. Take each one of these and ask why it's working.

During one of my seminars a participant had this exact list of things that he felt were working to grow his personal coaching practice. I wrote his list on the board in front of the room and asked him the second question. When I asked why "networking and word of mouth" were working, he replied because he was a good coach, people liked him, and they were willing tell others about his services.

Next on his list was "brochure." When I asked him why this was working an interesting thing happened. He began to realize that, while he assumed it was because he had an expensive brochure, the reality was that it had not brought him a single client. The same was true for his website. In reality, all his business was coming from his referral base. The brochure and website were only giving him the illusion that they were providing a result for him. This is a valuable step because it can guide you where to place your efforts and expenditures.

2. *What does the ideal look like?*

This is where you get to really see the vision of what is possible. For my coach friend, the ideal vision was having a steady stream of satisfied clients being referred to him and having a waiting list of people who wanted to work with him.

3. *What's not quite right yet?*

Notice I did not say, "What's wrong?" We're not going to go there. By using the phrase, "What's not quite right?" you are presupposing that all it needs is an adjustment to be right. By adding the word "yet" you are establishing that it will be.

In our coach's case what was not quite right was that, in reality, he had few clients. This is a very significant step because it identifies the gap between your desire and your current reality. If you refer back to the section about bridge beliefs, you will see that is a situation where you could create a bridge belief to help you reach your goal.

4. *What resources do I need?*

This question identifies who can help and what you need to do to reach your goal. In the case of our coach friend, he saw that by expanding his referral base, he would build his business. We were then able to brainstorm ways in which he could do that.

Let's look at how you could apply this to another area of your life. Supposing you want to focus more on your health.

What's working? might include things like eating a healthy diet, exercising, having a health screening, and so on. If you took "eating a healthy diet," for example, and asked *Why is it working?* you might list that you're eating less fat and sugar and more fresh fruits and vegetables. The ideal vision might be a diet totally composed of healthy foods.

What's not quite right yet? may be that you still eat a lot of less-than-healthy foods high in fat, calories, and sugar.

What resources do I need? might include making an appointment with a nutritionist or personal trainer.

By following this simple five-question format you have established a clear picture of the situation, uncovered what is working and why, identified what is not quite right yet and the help you need. You have also begun to create a plan to help you move further along toward your goal.

Treasure Maps

In What Are You Waiting For? It's Your Life (Sound Wisdom, 2013), I wrote about "treasure maps" as an aid to manifesting your dreams and desires. This is one of the most powerful visual aids you can employ and is well worth explaining in more detail here.

The first time I used a *treasure map*, sometimes referred to as *dream board* or *vision board*, was many years ago when I was beginning to rebuild my life. At the time I owned an old, beat-up car. Actually that is an understatement. It was a twelve-year-old hunk of metal that barely ran. It had a vinyl top, but most of the vinyl was worn away and what was left was peeling. There was a hole in the floor on the driver's side that let cold wind in during the winter. I used to place my foot over it. The paint was fading and it did not run very well. My wife, who I was dating at the time, did not even want to ride in it. Whenever we went out we took her luxury car.

My goal at the time was a new, top-of-the-line Honda Accord. Knowing about the power of treasure maps, I had visited the Honda dealer and obtained a brochure of the car I wanted. In addition to having a written goal of driving the new Honda,

I placed a picture on the wall above my desk where I would see it throughout the day.

One day I took the picture down because the car was in my driveway. I owned a new Accord. Please do not misunderstand—I am not suggesting that this just happened by itself. The car dealer did not drive by my house looking for someone to give the car to. I had to do certain things to improve my life to be in a position to make it possible. The treasure map helped speed things up by consistently imprinting on my subconscious mind an image of my desire.

Whatever you want to have in your life, use visuals to help your subconscious see what it is that you want. For example, if you want to go on a fabulous vacation to Hawaii, get some travel brochures and make a collage of the pictures of beach scenes, hotels, and other images that will give you visual reinforcement for your goal. Be sure to include pictures of yourself and family in your *treasure map*.

When we were looking for our current home in Bucks County, Pennsylvania, I created a *treasure map* using a picture of Georgia and myself, pictures of Bucks County, a headline that said "Bucks County Pennsylvania," ads for homes, and a picture of the kind of house we wanted. I wrote phrases and affirmations on it as well and hung it where we would see it daily. This helped reinforce our goal in our minds and helped bring it to us.

Visual aids are very powerful; if you doubt this just look at the impact television has had on people's buying habits. The next time you look at a magazine, notice how much more powerful the ads with photos are compared to those with just text. You too can use the power of the visual media to help you obtain what you want.

Creation Box

Another variation along the same line as a treasure map is something called a creation box. To use this idea, simply obtain a box of whatever size you feel is appropriate. As you read through newspapers, magazines, and catalogues, notice the pictures of the things that you would like to attract into your own life. They may be material things like cameras, computers, automobiles, furniture, or they can be emotional states like joy, peace, and serenity. When you see a picture, particularly something that you would like to have, a place you would like to visit, or an emotional state that you would like to experience, cut it out and, after looking at it closely, place it in your creation box. You can even write on slips of paper things that you want to have or emotional states that you would like to experience more regularly.

As with the treasure map, you are once again teaching your conscious and subconscious mind what you would like to have or experience in your life. You are, in effect, actively creating your life as you live it.

Our subconscious mind records everything that occurs in our lives. This has been validated using hypnosis. People who have been hypnotized have been able to recall many years in the past with great detail. Your subconscious mind will record and remember the fact that you chose specific things and affirmed your desire to have them in your life. This will reinforce your intention and help you move more quickly toward your desires.

From time to time you can revisit your creation box to reinforce these ideas. I have found, over time, that when I go back to look at my creation box, I already have many of its contents in my life. It occurred as if by magic!

Making the Most of Your Time

I'm certain that you will agree that we all live very busy lives. Furthermore, you will also agree that we are living a hectic pace, and it's all we can do just to keep up with the demands placed upon us by modern living.

Many young couples are balancing careers or businesses with raising families and caring for their children and older parents, while at the same time trying to find a little time for themselves. Add to this, time for running household errands, shopping for groceries, and many other tasks we all do to keep our lives moving along, and it can be overwhelming.

We have friends who, in addition to their own high-powered careers, are raising two teenagers. With all the activities available to today's teens, just keeping up with them is almost a full-time job. Another friend of ours has a fourteen-year-old son who plays nine different sports, each with its own practice and game schedule, not to mention equipment. So how do we not only cope and maintain balance, but even thrive in all of this?

I believe, and there is plenty empirical evidence to support it, that time management and preplanning is one of the keys. The time that you devote to planning your week and day will pay for itself many times over.

Whether you use a notebook or journal, paper-based planner or tablet, it is crucial to your success and well-being to invest time in planning your activities. I noticed when I began adding my exercise time to my daily plan that, instead of trying to squeeze it in as I went along, I was there at the appointed time and on track to reach my health goals.

I sometimes even schedule time to go out with my wife on a "date." This has become increasingly important as I become busier and am asked to do more speaking. By scheduling our "date night," usually a Friday, I know I will not, if at all possible, make any other commitments. If I do, I will schedule our date on another evening. Often the things that are most important to us tend to become squeezed into whatever time is left over. We lose out on the things that we most want to do as a result of not planning our day.

A while back I noticed that my writing time, something that for me is the most important activity I do and the one I enjoy most, was being relegated to "fit in" where possible. I began scheduling time to write. As a result I have become even more productive and am enjoying it more.

One of the secrets to a balanced life I learned from my friend, Jim Sutton. When I asked him how he managed to be exercising every morning, being an attorney with a very busy practice, he replied, "I make it one of my top three things to do each day." Notice he did not say one of my top ten. By putting the really important activities on your schedule first, you will ensure they're being completed.

If you take care of the "big rocks" first, you can always find the time for the smaller ones.

What are your most important three to five daily tasks and activities? For me, writing and exercise are scheduled first; I then look at my other tasks and schedule time for the other top two or three. In the remaining time I do the less important things that we all need to do.

When you look at your weekly or monthly plan, do you see time for self-care and relaxation? If not, ask yourself if this is really how you want to live.

Activity: Planning Your Time

To be sure that you keep balance in your life, when you are doing your monthly, weekly, or daily plan have your goals nearby. If you make sure that you regularly plan something in each area—spiritual, health, career, etc.—you will be in balance and alignment with your major goals.

In our busy, complex society, it is too easy to become caught up in the pace of daily living, only to wake up ten years in the future realizing you're not where you want to be. An investment of a small amount of time monthly, weekly and daily to plan your activities will help you achieve more of what you want in your life.

Being Watchful for Opportunities

Many of what we know today as successful enterprises were actually born out of frustration and need. Opportunities are all around us, all we need to do is begin to pay attention to our surroundings. What do people around you seem to want that they are not getting?

In 1980, Gerald Aul, Pat Senn, and Robert Diaz began observing that people were frustrated at the lack of the services being provided by the post office and asked, "Why can't people just come in and have merchandise packed and shipped without having to do it all themselves?" This simple question, combined with the frustration they and others were experiencing, led to the start of Mail Boxes, Etc. At last count the company, now part of UPS, has more than 4,000 locations worldwide.

Another successful global company born out of a simple need is the Honda Corporation. In the years following World War II, with gasoline in short supply, most Japanese were using bicycles as their main form of transportation. Wanting to make it easier for his countrymen to move around, Soichiro Honda invented a small engine that attached to the bicycle enabling it to go faster while still conserving fuel. This little engine was the beginning of the Honda Corporation.

Barney, the big, loveable, purple dinosaur, who entertains children all over the world, was developed because its creator was not able to find video programs that she felt were suitable for her young child.

YouTube was born out of a desire to be able to share videos online. The rest, as they say, is history.

What are the opportunities that surround you? One way to uncover these is to pay attention to what people are saying. What do people seem to want that is not available?

If you are a part of your local business community, what opportunities are right in front of you? For example, if you hear several people talking about how they need help with social media and you know someone who offers this service, you might ask for a small referral fee for introducing them to a new client. You could even act as a free agent, representing one or more local service businesses. If you pay attention, there are always simple, ethical, legal ways you can increase your income, especially in today's global business environment.

Success Leaves Clues

If you want to become more successful in any area of your life, make a habit of studying successful people. Taking charge of your destiny and living the life you were born to live is not something that you have to figure out on your own.

In addition to the ideas, tools, and techniques discussed in this book, libraries and bookstores are filled with wonderful books as well as audio programs to help you along your path. Make a habit of reading good books and listening to podcasts and audio programs.

Attend seminars whenever possible. Not only will you expand your mind, you will be in a position to meet and get to know like-minded people. Remember what I said earlier about hanging out with the winners. Develop relationships with other positive people who, like you, want the best life they are capable of achieving.

Make it a practice to read biographies of people you admire and people who have excelled in their life. In doing this you will begin to see the patterns and gain insight into what these people did to succeed.

If succeeding in business is something that interests you, read biographies of people like Benjamin Franklin; Sam Walton, founder of Wal-Mart;

Bill Gates, founder of Microsoft; Soichiro Honda, founder of Honda; Sakichi Toyota, founder of Toyota; Akio Morita, founder of Sony; Ray Kroc, founder of McDonalds; Thomas Edison, inventor of the light bulb; Howard Schultz, founder of Starbucks; Henry Ford, founder of the Ford Motor Company; Mary Kay Ash, founder of Mary Kay Cosmetics, and other successful business people. In their biographies you will learn what steps they took, how they thought, and most important of all you will read about the adversity they overcame to reach their goals. You will learn that no matter what happened, each of these highly successful people persevered until they succeeded. Giving up was never an issue. Failure was viewed as a temporary setback and learning experience.

Conclusion

"Winners are those people who make a habit of doing the things losers are uncomfortable doing."

—ED FORMAN

*C*ongratulations! You have just completed a major step in taking charge of your destiny and creating the life you were born to live.

If you've skipped any of the activities, please go back and complete them now. Within you is the power to change your life and the simple, easy-to-follow activities in this book have been developed to assist you tapping into that power to create the life of you want.

You may want to go back and re-read sections, taking notes along the way. You can use these to remind you of the key points that have helped you. Each time we read something, we understand it a little differently, so re-reading is always a worthwhile activity.

Of course, you'll want to continue your personal development program beyond this book. Making personal growth a lifelong endeavor will reward you in untold ways. You can learn more about my other books, programs, and services at www.jimdonovan.com.

Commit now to a steady diet of positive, uplifting information. Devote some time each day to reading books and listening to podcasts and audio programs that will help you stay on the right track to create your magical life.

Remember the lesson from the timeless James Allen book, *As a Man Thinketh*. In it he says our minds are like a garden—if we do not plant the seeds of positive ideas, weeds will grow by themselves.

Populate your garden with the seeds of inspiring ideas. Nurture them, act on them, and watch them blossom into the life you were born to live.

My sincere best wishes for a joyous, successful, and productive life and that you use your success in an enlightened way, helping to make our world a better place for all.

Be well and God bless,

JIM DONOVAN
Bucks County, Pennsylvania

About Jim Donovan

Jim Donovan, who for more than twenty years has been a speaker and a coach, is a recognized thought leader in the field of personal development. In addition, his books and teachings have positively impacted the lives of millions of people throughout the world.

Speaking openly about his pain and struggle, what he calls his "decade of destruction," and sharing the ideas and techniques that enabled him to radically change his life have made him a sought-after speaker and trainer for business events and meetings. Jim's unique sense of humor, coupled with his varied life experiences, allows him to connect with people from all walks of life.

Several of his books have been international bestsellers, bringing his message of hope and possibility to people everywhere. Jim's articles have appeared in numerous print and digital magazines, and he is a frequent media guest and expert source on human performance and personal development.

His *Jim's Jems* e-zine has been published online since 1992. A free subscription and complimentary gift are available at his website, www.JimDonovan.com.

Jim, a native New Yorker, now enjoys what he considers the best of all worlds—living with his wife, Georgia, their cats, and a myriad of wild animals in a beautiful wooded area of upper Bucks County, Pennsylvania.

OTHER BOOKS BY JIM DONOVAN

Happy at Work:
60 Simple Ways to Stay Engaged and Be Successful

What Are You Waiting For? It's Your Life

Handbook to a Happier Life

Available in book stores or
from www.JimDonovan.com.

Visit www.jimdonovan.com/gift to sign up for a free subscription to *Jim's Jems* e-zine for personal and professional growth. Published since 1992, it is read by individuals and business people throughout the world.

To inquire about Jim Donovan speaking at your next event or to learn more about working with him or for any other information, please email Jim@jimdonovan.com.